Prayer

A Guide for Leaders, Parents and Teachers

Lenny La Guardia

Forerunner Books
Kansas City, Missouri

Prayer: A Guide for Leaders, Parents and Teachers
By Lenny La Guardia
Children's Equipping Center
International House of Prayer

Published by Forerunner Books
International House of Prayer
3535 East Red Bridge Road
Kansas City, Missouri 64137
(816) 763-0200 Ext. 2675
forerunnerbooks@ihop.org
www.IHOP.org

Copyright © 2007 by Forerunner Books and the Children's Equipping Center
All rights reserved.

This book or parts of this book may not be reproduced in any form, stored in a retrieval system, or transmitted in any form by any means—electronic, mechanical, photocopy, recording, or otherwise—without prior written permission of the publisher, except as provided by United States of America copyright law.

ISBN: 0-978-0-9755625-7-4

Unless otherwise noted, all Scripture quotations are from the New King James Version of the Bible. Copyright © 1979, 1980, 1982 by Thomas Nelson, Inc., publishers.

Cover design by Tom Morse-Brown
Interior design by Dale Jimmo

Printed in the United States of America

Table of Contents

Welcome 5

Introduction 7

Lesson One: Letting God Unlock Our Hearts 13

Lesson Two: We Are Known By God 23

Lesson Three: God's Glad Heart 33

Lesson Four: One Thing 43

Lesson Five: Thy Kingdom Come 55

Lesson Six: God's Goodness Sustains Our Hearts 65

Lesson Seven: His Name Is Great Among All the Nations 75

Lesson Eight: Who Is Like You, O God? 85

Lesson Nine: Giving Thanks to God 95

Lesson Ten: Jesus: The Lamb of God 105

Song Lyrics 115

Age Group Characteristics and Communication Tips 127

About the Children's Equipping Center 137

Children's Equipping Center Annual Events 139

Welcome and Thank You!

Greetings!

Thank you for making *Prayer* and the Glad Heart Resource Series a part of your life and the lives of those you teach and reach for God. At the International House of Prayer (IHOP–KC) Missions Base and the Children's Equipping Center, one of our highest goals is to see young people today grounded in the Word of God and released in praise, prayer, power and the prophetic. As a part of this series, *Prayer* endeavors to assist you as you encourage, teach, parent, and lead a generation into an understanding of prayer and intercession. We believe that bringing together the music and the message will aid you in the pursuit of fresh revelation of God's heart for them, encouraging them to place themselves before Him in prayer, regardless of their circumstances.

We have ministered to young people for twenty-five years. We see today, more than at any other time, the massive need for a paradigm shift—a change in the way we view this ministry—for that greatly influences how we choose resources and prepare and present lessons to our children and those we lead.

Long ago, one of our mentors taught us that the definition of curriculum was derived from the Latin term meaning "course of ground." To understand the purpose of curricula, we must understand the course of ground that God would have us cover with this generation of children. As you prepare your lesson each week, keep in mind the course of ground you will be covering with your students and have a destination or goal set before you begin.

Over the course of these many years spent serving families, we have always believed that the strongest curricula and workbooks ever written come directly from the Word of God. In developing the Glad Heart Resource Series, we have adhered to that belief and have set out to help young people, their parents and leaders obtain godly understanding of theological truth that unlocks the human heart to the reality that God delights in us and desires to have an intimate relationship with us.

We believe that God desires to give us and you fresh vision for equipping a generation of young people to walk in His truth with the spirit of relational prayer and intercession as a primary motivating factor.

May the Lord continue to give you grace as you pursue one of the greatest privileges we can have while walking with Jesus: teaching young people.

Blessings in the Name of the Lord,

Lenny and Tracy La Guardia

Introduction

Bringing the Music and Message Together

The Glad Heart Resource Series introduces and explores four primary themes, one in each book. The four themes are as follows:

- **Praise:** Ten lessons and ten songs to teach young people to give God praise, no matter what circumstances surround them. King David described the three responses of people who fear God and put their trust in Him alone: they tremble, rejoice, and embrace the heart of God (Psalm 2:2–12).

- **Prayer:** Ten lessons and ten songs to teach young people the reality of God's unconditional love for them and His desire to have an on-going personal relationship with them. Isaiah 56:7 says, "I will bring them to My holy mountain and make them joyful in My house of prayer for all nations."

- **Power:** Ten lessons and ten songs that provide young people with an understanding of the truth of God's desire for them to walk in the power of the Holy Spirit by revealing salvation to the lost, preaching the Gospel, healing the sick and broken-hearted, and ministering to the poor. Isaiah 8:18 says, "Here am I and the children whom the Lord has given me! We are for signs and wonders."

- **Prophetic:** Ten lessons and ten songs to teach young people how to develop godly character and understand why and how God speaks to them and through them. Acts 2:17 tells us that, in the last days, God's Spirit will be poured out on all flesh and that His sons and daughters will prophesy.

Understanding the Glad Heart Resource Series: Prayer

Each lesson includes a corresponding song on the accompanying CD, making one complete lesson. You, the teacher, will be involved in the following five steps that will assist you in presenting the lessons with passion and clarity. (We also believe that you will find it helpful to concurrently complete Mike Bickle's Song of Solomon series, which contains teaching on the subject of relational prayer.)

1. **Reflect** on the theme of *Prayer* by completing the personal reflection section prior to preparing each of the ten lessons that support the theme. This section will aid you in getting in touch with your own heart and the hearts of the students.

2. **Listen** to the song that goes with each lesson several times, and journal your thoughts and reflections in the template provided. These notes can be used in the teaching.

3. **Review** the background information about the song to see why it was chosen to be part of that lesson. This will help you become acquainted with the heart of the song so that you feel confident discussing it with your students. Remember, we don't want our young people just going through the motions when they sing; we want them to take the songs seriously and, through them, be led to a place of prayer and intercession.

4. **Study** and meditate on the biblical content presented in each lesson and examine the lesson objective. This allows you to gain the biblical understanding and revelation needed to soundly communicate the Word of God.

5. **Complete** the lesson template as you prepare to teach the biblical content and objective. This gives you an action plan.

Personal Reflection on the Theme of "Prayer"

This section will assist you in being open and honest and, most of all, approachable to your children and students. Young people desire us to be vulnerable and transparent, and we need to open up our hearts and lives to this generation. Many of our most important times of communicating to young people come when we share personal experiences and areas that are a little tender to us.

Please review the statements and answer the personal reflection questions. Put your heart into this, and focus on bringing out your true thoughts. Write your responses to the statements below in the space provided.

- Who modeled prayer to you when you were a child, and who has impacted your life the most in the area of prayer?

- Today, more than ever, young people tend to view prayer as boring. It has become a routine before meals, sporting events, or going to bed. For many, it has been reduced to simply asking God to bless something or someone important to us. How have you viewed prayer, its value and purpose?

- What has been tugging on your heart regarding what young people see and face today, what they experience, etc.?

- Lines of communication are often shut down as a result of disappointment and hurt within our relationships. It is not uncommon for this to happen in prayer as well. Sometimes life seems like too much to bear, so we turn on God and blame Him for what has happened or is happening.

  What was the most hurtful time in your life? Is that area still tender? If not, how did you get through it?

  Have you ever cut off communication with someone you love? If so, when and with whom?

- When some people turn away from God, they never understand why the walls in their hearts grow bigger and thicker. Theses walls are the ways that we hide our true feelings and try to keep from connecting with others so that we don't get hurt anymore.

In what areas of your life have you allowed walls to go up?

- It is our hope that as you deliver the message of the Gospel, you do so with love and kindness.

  In the past, when have your words been harsh, or when have you been impatient with the young people you were teaching?

- Many young people have deep, personal heart wounds from role models who have not demonstrated the love of Jesus with tenderness and integrity.

  What is your idea of a good role model? What areas within working with young people cause you the most frustration and why? Pray and give these areas over to God.

- As a communicator of the theme of prayer, it is important that you embrace what God desires to show you about prayer. He can help you teach a generation His heart for us to pray.

  Write about an occasion when you stepped in during a time of crisis, conflict, or concern, contending for a much-needed breakthrough.

- God's love for us goes deep, and nothing will stop Him from loving us.

  How would you rate and describe your understanding of God's love?

- This manual is intended to help you and your students unlock your hearts in the area of prayer. We want young people and those of us who teach them to set our eyes on the Lord even when the world around us is full of change, pain, and turmoil. For years, much of the Church has indirectly taught children that prayer is good and important, but never revealed the power of a relational God who not only speaks to His children but hears and saves every word that is spoken in prayer. *Prayer* is designed to explore the heart of God and release young people and teachers to grow in intimacy with God.

  Write in your journal about how God has changed your understanding of prayer over the last several years. Do you feel that you have come to the place of giving Him your words no matter what circumstances surround you? Describe what happened in your heart. If you are still working toward that, write about the journey you're on—where you've come from and where you feel that you are heading. Then, do the following exercise.

- Make a list of every person to whom you will teach this material.

- Next to each name, write what you know about that person.

- Write how you believe each of them sees you as a person and as a teacher.

- Write down the changes you plan to make in relating to and communicating with them as a result of this personal evaluation.

- Write one thing for which you will pray daily or weekly for each person.

- Identify the difficulties each has experienced or is experiencing now.

- Ask God to show you His heart for each child.

Understanding the Lesson

The preparation and presentation section of each lesson has the following three components:

1. **The Invitation: Into the Heart of God** is designed to invite you and your students into the heart of God, the lesson objective, and the message of the corresponding song. This section gives you an opportunity to examine your own heart and to consider how the lesson theme and song can impact your life. Our ministries are only as strong as our personal devotion to the Lord.

2. **The Impartation: Into the Knowledge of God.** This component will help you understand the Word of God and personally apply the biblical content so you can teach each lesson objective with authority and passion.

3. **The Lesson Presentation Template** will assist you in developing an action plan and preparing to communicate each lesson in your own words, integrating the biblical text and the song. The Lesson Presentation Template includes the following concepts:

   - **The Invitation:** Share with your students your heart for them to embrace the lesson you will be teaching. Become transparent and available. Communicate your desire for them to experience from the lesson the heart and love God has for them.

   - **The Impartation:** Invite your students into the knowledge of God through His Word.

   - **The Application: Applying the Truth to Our Lives.** Use the template to prepare your heart and mind for the lesson and to create an action plan for teaching it.

   - **The Impact: Letting God Have All of Us.** Do the exercises before teaching in order to guide the students as they write out their own thoughts. The exercises are designed to enable them to apply what they have learned in the lesson to impact and influence their family, friends, schools, neighborhoods and the nations for God.

LESSON 1: Letting God Unlock Our Hearts

Biblical Foundation: Zephaniah 3:17 and Psalm 139:17–18
Song: "Song of Joy"

Objective: To assist the students in obtaining a better understanding that God desires to speak to us and define us according to His vision, heart and Word. This lesson is designed to help foster knowledge of who we are in Christ by believing what He says about us and experiencing joy that comes only by knowing His love. We will learn the importance of shutting out the paralyzing voices around us that can lock up our hearts from receiving God's gladness. Confidence in His love produces prayers of thanksgiving.

Resource Materials Needed:

- *Prayer* CD
- Sound system to play the CD
- Handouts of the lyrics to "Song of Joy"
- Your Bible and a Bible for each student
- Your journal and a journal for each student
- Handouts of the Apostolic Prayers

I. The Invitation: Into the Heart of God

This step will assist you in preparing to bring the heart of the message together with the heart of the music, while embracing God's heart for the students you will be teaching.

A. Listen to "Song of Joy" several times.

B. As you listen to the song, write in your journal the key phrases and lyrics that impact you the most.

C. Pray and mediate on these key phrases, letting God unlock your heart to receive the truth of how He feels about you.

II. The Impartation: Into the Knowledge of God

This step will help you understand why the song was written and identify the main points to communicate from it. It will also help you gain insight into the biblical foundations of the lesson and the song as you consider the truths contained in each.

A. Main points to the song

　　1. The lyrics of "Song of Joy" attempt to communicate the truth that He rejoices over us with singing, and His love for us is never-ending. This song will help us push aside the influences and voices that try to break us down and make us feel that we have no destiny, hope, or purpose.

　　2. Knowing how God feels about us can help us keep our eyes off of ourselves and our circumstances and set our gaze on Him. Sometimes we need to ask ourselves if we know who God is in the midst of crisis, rejection and other painful emotions. This song helps us reflect on the sustaining beauty of God, which is ever-present.

　　3. This song encourages us to ask the Lord to let us hear the song He is singing over us: words of love and words of joy. Many voices come to us through the form of media (TV, Internet, magazines, etc.), telling us what we need to look like (or not look like) and how we should act or feel. As children of God, it is His voice to which we should incline our ear.

　　4. Hearing the song He sings over us can cause a change in our lives as we allow the Lord to unlock our hearts. We will grow in confidence and faith in God when we become rooted in His love. Others' opinions of us will not matter, compared to what God says and thinks about us; His opinion is the only one that matters.

B. Biblical Foundation: Read, study, and meditate on Zephaniah 3:17 and Psalm 139:17–18.

The LORD your God in your midst, the Mighty One, will save; He will rejoice over you with gladness, He will quiet you with His love, He will rejoice over you with singing. (Zephaniah 3:17)

Key Points to Remember

　　1. Zephaniah prophesied in the days of Josiah, king of Judah. He greatly influenced Josiah's leadership, providing support to the young king.

Josiah brought about great reformation and restored true worship in Jerusalem.

2. Zephaniah prophesied during a time when the people of Judah were not living according to God's law. He spoke of the time of exile that was coming as a result of their behavior.

3. Chapters 1 and 2 of the book of Zephaniah reveal the impending judgment for Judah and for the nations. While it may seem that God had forsaken them, Zephaniah speaks of a remnant being saved (2:3,7, 3:12–13) and of their return from captivity (2:7, 3:20).

4. Chapter 3 assures the people that God will restore the remnant and fulfill all of His promises. This chapter reveals God's true emotions toward us. It is the perfect revelation of God to man: a joyful nation singing glad songs of redemption, and all the earth resounding with the praise of God's people.

How precious also are your thoughts to me, O God! How great is the sum of them! If I should count them, they would be more in number than the sand; When I awake, I am still with you. (Psalm 139:17–18)

Key Points to Remember

1. In this Psalm of thanksgiving, David speaks of God's presence and infinite knowledge. He is reflecting on how precious God's thoughts are to him.

2. Verses 17–18 reference the many thoughts of God and how He shares them with men. David is overwhelmed by the fact that there are too many thoughts to even count.

3. Nothing is hidden from God, yet nothing can remove His love for us nor His desire to reveal Himself and communicate His thoughts to us.

III. Preparation: Action Plan and Lesson Presentation Template

This step will help you develop an action plan to communicate the lesson using a template. This presentation template has been designed to assist you in organizing and presenting the material in the most effective manner.

Bear in mind all that you have considered and learned by contemplating the song and studying the lesson.

We, as teachers, are to serve our students; they are not to serve us. Remember that we do so in order that they may in turn serve God with a greater understanding of His ways in their lives. Be sensitive to the needs of the students, keeping in mind that God is faithful and good and knows them better than anyone. Use the " S.E.R.V.A.N.T." method.

"S.E.R.V.A.N.T." spelled out is:

S: "Share"—Share your life with your students.

E: "Example"—Be an example of the truth to them.

R: "Represent"—Represent Christ correctly to your students.

V: "Voice"—Help them learn to recognize God's voice.

A: "Authority"—Teach in the power of God with His authority.

N: "Needs"—Meet the needs of your students so that God is glorified.

T: "Train and Teach"—As you train and teach, do so rightly dividing the Word of God.

Prayer

Lesson Presentation Template

Theme: Prayer

Lesson: "Letting God Unlock Your Heart"

Lesson Biblical Foundation: Zephaniah 3:17 and Psalm 139:17–18

Song: "Song of Joy"

PART ONE: The Invitation

In this section, you will invite your students to know your heart for them to embrace the lesson you are teaching. Be transparent and reachable. Communicate your desire for them to experience from the lesson the heart and love God has for them.

A. Play "Song of Joy" several times.

B. Have the students write down in their journals what they think are the key points of the song. Ask them to write down how these parts of the song speak to them about God.

C. Share the background about the song and the messages the songwriter desires to convey.

D. Share your responses to the following questions.

   a. Has it been difficult for you to open your heart to receive God's love? Have you had trouble believing the truth that His thoughts toward you are happy ones?

   b. How has that changed since studying this lesson? How can you best explain these changes?

   c. What changes have you made or will make in your own life that you are comfortable sharing with your students?

   d. Spend a few minutes sharing about the heart God has given you for your students. Choose a portion of Scripture from the Apostolic Prayers handout and pray it over them.

PART TWO: The Impartation

In this section, you will invite the students into the knowledge of God through His Word.

A. Have the students open their Bibles. Read Zephaniah 3:17 and Psalm 139:17–18 with them.

B. Begin a dialog by asking them to give their thoughts about the messages conveyed in these passages.

C. Based on these passages, identify together at least five ways God will show us His thoughts and His love toward us.

- Point #1:

- Point #2:

- Point #3:

- Point #4:

- Point #5:

D. Identify at least three attributes of God that, when we remember them, will sustain our hearts in difficult times.

- Point #1:

- Point #2:

- Point #3:

PART THREE: The Application

In this section, you will help the students identify areas of their lives where they can apply God's Word and experience His emotions.

Note: They should have their journals with them and be prepared to write in them.

A. Ask the students to identify and write in their journals how they felt God saw them before reading and studying Zephaniah 3:17 and Psalm 139:17–18.

B. Ask the students to identify and write in their journals a positive thought that one of their parents has toward them. Then discuss how much more God delights in us.

C. Ask the students to identify and write in their journals areas in their lives where they have paid attention to negative influences.

D. Ask the students to identify and write in their journals what areas in their lives are currently controlling them. Give some examples.

E. Ask the students to consider how a relationship with God is meant to sustain and comfort them and help them overcome difficulties and struggles.

PART FOUR: The Impact

A. Play the song again. Give a copy of the lyrics to each student, and ask them to sing along.

B. Ask the students to sit quietly and reflect on God's great love for them. Ask them to give this time over to the Lord by letting God into all areas of their lives.

C. Explain to your students that God wants to reveal His thoughts to us. Pray an example prayer of thanksgiving for this. Have the students spend at least five minutes in prayer, thanking God for the thoughts and love that He has for us.

D. Print this prayer and give a copy to each student. Pray it together out loud.

Thank you, God, for sending Your only Son to Earth to die for my sins. Thank you that You did that because You love me. Help me to remember that You have many, many thoughts toward me and that they are all glad and joyful.

Please help me to hear the song of joy that You sing over my life. Holy Spirit, help me to pray with as much joy as the Father has. Whether I am having a good day or a bad day, I want to be joyful because I know that You love me.

I close the door to the areas in my life where Satan has had a grip. I ask, God, that through the power of the Holy Spirit, You would give me strength to put all my concerns, hurts and trials into Your hands and trust Jesus as my Savior and Lord. In Jesus' name, amen.

E. Invite the Holy Spirit to visit your students, and ask if there is anyone who would like individual prayer. Pray for them, and ask others to join you in praying for them when appropriate.

Prayer

Student Journal and Notes

_____

_____

_____

_____

_____

_____

_____

_____

_____

_____

_____

_____

_____

LESSON TWO: We Are Known By God

Biblical Foundation: Ephesians 1:3–6
Song: "Before the World Began"

Objective: To introduce the children to the reality that God knew us, loved us and chose us to be adopted into His family even before the creation of the world.

Resource Materials Needed:

- *Prayer* CD
- Sound system to play the CD
- Handouts of the lyrics to "Before the World Began"
- Your Bible and a Bible for each student
- Your journal and a journal for each student
- Handouts of the Apostolic Prayers

I.   The Invitation: Into the Heart of God

This step will assist you in preparing to bring the heart of the message together with the heart of the music, while embracing God's heart for the students you will be teaching.

A. Listen to "Before the World Began" several times.

B. As you listen to the song, write in your journal the key phrases and lyrics from the song that impact you the most.

C. Reflect and meditate on these key phrases.

II. The Impartation: Into the Knowledge of God

This step will help you understand why the song was written and identify the main points to communicate from it. It will also help you gain insight into the biblical foundations of the lesson and the song as you consider the truths contained in each.

A. Main points to the song "Before the World Began"

1. This song was written to communicate the truth that God knew us even before the world began.

2. It encourages us to reflect on the provision He made for our redemption before we were even created. He demonstrated His love for us before we were even born.

3. This song encourages us in the knowledge that we can always ask Him to let us experience more of His love.

4. "Before the World Began" was written to help us be thankful and remember that He created the earth for our pleasure.

5. This song will help us enter into a new dimension of joy, realizing that we are more than a number, or just one face among millions. God knows each of us by name, and He takes great delight in us.

B. Biblical Foundation: Read, study, and meditate on Ephesians 1:3–6.

Blessed be the God and Father of our Lord Jesus Christ, who has blessed us with every spiritual blessing in the heavenly places in Christ, just as He chose us in Him before the foundation of the world, that we should be holy and without blame before Him in love, having predestined us to adoption as sons by Jesus Christ to Himself, according to the good pleasure of His will, to the praise of the glory of His grace, by which He made us accepted in the Beloved.

Key Points to Remember

1. Paul is addressing both Gentile and Jewish believers. In this passage, he is not making a point as much as he is praising God for gift after gift, wonder after wonder.

2. God blesses us with that which can only be found in Heaven and cannot be obtained by man or from man.

3. Paul states that God chose us. When we look at the goodness of God, it is no wonder that we chose Him; the wonder lies in the fact that God chose us.

4. Verse 5 speaks of how God always planned that we would be a part of His family, that we would be children of God and joint heirs with Christ.

III. Preparation: Action Plan and Lesson Presentation Template

This step will help you develop an action plan to communicate the lesson using a template. This presentation template has been designed to assist you in organizing and presenting the material in the most effective manner.

Bear in mind all that you have considered and learned by contemplating the song and studying the lesson.

We, as teachers, are to serve our students; they are not to serve us. Remember that we do so in order that they may in turn serve God with a greater understanding of His ways in their lives. Be sensitive to the needs of the students, keeping in mind that God is faithful and good and knows them best.

"S.E.R.V.A.N.T." spelled out is:

S: "Share"—Share your life with your students.

E: "Example"—Be an example of the truth to them.

R: "Represent"—Represent Christ correctly to your students.

V: "Voice"—Help them learn to recognize God's voice.

A: "Authority"—Teach in the power of God with His authority.

N: "Needs"—Meet the needs of your students so that God is glorified.

T: "Train and Teach"—As you train and teach, do so rightly dividing the Word of God.

Lesson Presentation Template

Theme: Prayer

Lesson: "We are Known by God"

Lesson Biblical Foundation: Ephesians 1:3–6

Song: "Before the World Began"

PART ONE: The Invitation

In this section, you will invite your students to know your heart for them to embrace the lesson you are teaching. Be transparent and reachable. Communicate your desire for them to experience from the lesson the heart and love God has for them.

   A. Play "Before the World Began" several times.

   B. Have the students write down what they think are the key points of the song. Ask them to write down parts of the song that speak to them about God.

   C. Share with your students your responses to the following questions.

      a. Have there been times in your life when you felt like God has forgotten you? If so, write down your experience and share it with your students.

      b. How has studying this lesson impacted the way you feel about God's love toward you?

      c. How can you best explain this impact?

      d. Do you feel like there are things in your life that should change in light of what you have studied in this lesson? If so, what are your plans? Share them with your students.

      e. Spend a few minutes sharing about the heart God has given you for your students. Choose a portion of Scripture from the Apostolic Prayers handout, and pray it over them.

PART TWO: The Impartation

In this section, you will invite the students into the knowledge of God through His Word.

A. Have the students open their Bibles. Read Ephesians 1:3–6 with them.

B. Begin a dialog by asking them to give their thoughts about what these verses tell us about the character of God.

C. Have your students identify three things that are true about God as seen in these verses.

- Truth #1:

- Truth #2:

- Truth #3:

D. Have your students identify three things about God that can sustain our hearts in difficult times.

- #1:

- #2:

- #3:

PART THREE: The Application

In this section, you will help the students identify areas of their lives where they can apply God's Word and experience His emotions.

Note: They should have their journals with them and be prepared to write in them.

A. Ask the students to identify and write in their journals how they feel about God knowing them.

B. Ask the students to journal the thoughts they have about knowing that God made provision for them to experience eternal life before they were created.

C. Ask the students to identify and write in their journals the areas in their lives in which they will ask the Lord to help them.

D. Ask the students to consider how a relationship with God is meant to sustain and comfort them and help them overcome difficulties and struggles.

PART FOUR: The Impact

A. Play the song again. Give a copy of the lyrics to each student, and ask them to sing along.

B. Explain to your students that God wants all of us to be with Him forever and that giving ourselves to prayer is a right response to His love.

C. Have the students write out a prayer acknowledging God for the blessings He has given them.

D. Print the following prayer, and give a copy to each student. Pray it together out loud.

Thank you, God, for sending Your only Son to die for my sins. Thank you that You made the way for me to be saved before I was born, even before You created the world.

I close the door to the areas in my life where Satan has had a grip. I ask, God, that through the power of the Holy Spirit, You would give me strength to put all my concerns, hurts and trials into Your hands and trust Jesus as my Savior and Lord.

Thank you for loving me the way that You do. God, I'm glad that You know me better than anyone else can. I want to know You better, too. Show me more about Yourself when I pray. In Jesus' name, amen.

E. Invite the Holy Spirit to visit your students, and ask if there is anyone who would like individual prayer. Pray for them, and ask others to join you in praying for them when appropriate.

Prayer

Student Journal and Notes

_____

_____

_____

_____

_____

_____

_____

_____

_____

_____

_____

_____

_____

_____

LESSON THREE: God's Glad Heart

Biblical Foundation: Romans 8:38–39 and Song of Solomon 2:4
Song: "Banqueting Table"

Objective: To help the students acquire the knowledge that God has invited us to walk with Christ and receive the blessings of His love and leadership. This lesson will also touch on how nothing formed against us can prosper if we abide in Christ and He in us.

Resource Materials Needed:

- *Prayer* CD
- Sound system to play the CD
- Handouts of the lyrics to "Banqueting Table"
- Your Bible and a Bible for each student
- Your journal and a journal for each student
- Handouts of the Apostolic Prayers

Prayer

I.   The Invitation: Into the Heart of God

This step will assist you in preparing to bring the heart of the message together with the heart of the music, while embracing the heart of God for the students you will be teaching.

A. Listen to "Banqueting Table" several times.

B. As you listen to the song, write in your journal the key phrases and lyrics from the song that impact you the most.

C. Reflect on what you think it means that He desires to bring you to His banqueting table. What do you think it means that His banner over you is love? Journal how it makes you feel to know that you are His beloved and His delight is in you.

D. Reflect on the positive leadership qualities of Jesus, and journal the ones you will attempt to model for those you lead and teach.

II. The Impartation: Into the Knowledge of God

This step will help you understand why the song was written and identify the main points to communicate from it. It will also help you gain insight into the biblical foundations of the lesson and the song as you consider the truths contained in each.

A. Main points to the song "Banqueting Table"

1. This song was incorporated in this theme because of its message of our identity in God as the beloved. His banner over us demonstrates the leadership and covering He desires to provide.

2. It encourages reflection on His perfect leadership. Acknowledging that His leadership cannot be improved upon, we see that even His discipline is for our good and produces fruit in our lives.

3. This song strengthens us in the knowledge that He delights in us and that we have been given an invitation to live in Christ as His Beloved.

4. Being invited to the banqueting table is a demonstration and celebration of God's unconditional love for us. This song helps us know that He desires to remove anything that gets in the way of our enjoying His love for us.

B. Biblical Foundation: Read, study, and meditate on Romans 8:38–39 and Song of Solomon 2:4.

For I am persuaded that neither death nor life, nor angels nor principalities nor powers, nor things present nor things to come, nor height nor depth, nor any other created thing, shall be able to separate us from the love of God which is in Christ Jesus our Lord. (Romans 8:38–39)

Key Points to Remember

1. In Romans 8, Paul writes about a new life in Christ that comes with the forgiveness of sin. He encourages us to be aware of the indwelling Holy Spirit who empowers us to walk with Jesus in the victory of His resurrection.

2. This chapter tells us of the victory we have over the flesh through life in the Spirit. Walking in the Spirit does not mean we will not be tempted; it means that we can access the Holy Spirit to draw us unto Jesus, the knowledge of His Word, and revelation of His character as a lover.

3. Verse 39 reveals to us God's mighty power that can defend us from all of the things that attempt to remove us from His love.

He brought me to His banqueting table, and His banner over me is love. (Song of Solomon 2:4)

Key Points to Remember

1. This verse speaks of the spiritual nourishment we receive from His presence. When we commune with Him, this leads us to rest in His joy.

2. The fullness of this celebration is at the marriage supper of the Lamb (Revelation 19:9). The church is referred to as the Bride of Christ throughout the New Testament. When Jesus returns, the Church's season of "engagement" will be over, and we will celebrate the wedding between He and His Bride.

3. His banner is the declaration of His love for the Bride in all of her life experiences. As the Bride of Christ, we can have the same confidence in God's love and mercy regardless of our circumstances.

III. Preparation: Action Plan and Lesson Presentation Template

This step will help you develop an action plan to communicate the lesson using a template. This presentation template has been designed to assist you in organizing and presenting the material in the most effective manner.

Bear in mind all that you have considered and learned by contemplating the song and studying the lesson.

We, as teachers, are to serve our students; they are not to serve us. Remember that we do so in order that they may in turn serve God with a greater understanding of His ways in their lives. Be sensitive to the needs of the students, keeping in mind that God is faithful and good and knows them best.

"S.E.R.V.A.N.T." spelled out is:

S: "Share"—Share your life with your students.

E: "Example"—Be an example of the truth to them.

R: "Represent"—Represent Christ correctly to your students.

V: "Voice"—Help them learn to recognize God's voice.

A: "Authority"—Teach in the power of God with His authority.

N: "Needs"—Meet the needs of your students so that God is glorified.

T: "Train and Teach"—As you train and teach, do so rightly dividing the Word of God.

Prayer

Lesson Presentation Template

Theme: Prayer

Lesson: "God's Glad Heart"

Lesson Biblical Foundation: Romans 8:38–39 and Song of Solomon 2:4

Song: "Banqueting Table"

PART ONE: The Invitation

In this section, you will invite your students to know your heart for them to embrace the lesson you are teaching. Be transparent and reachable. Communicate your desire for them to experience from the lesson the heart and love God has for them.

A. Play "Banqueting Table" several times.

B. Have the students write down what they think are the key points of the song. Ask them to write down the parts of the song that speak to them about God.

C. Share with your students your responses to the following questions.

   a. Have there been times in your life when you felt that God's love left you? If so, write down and share your experience.

   b. How did you get through that time until you could feel His love again?

   c. How has studying this lesson impacted the way you perceive God's love for you in times of difficulty?

   d. What changes do you need to make in your own life in light of this?

   e. Spend a few minutes sharing about the heart God has given you for your students. Choose a portion of Scripture from the Apostolic Prayer handout and pray it over them.

PART TWO: The Impartation

In this section, you will invite the students into the knowledge of God through His Word.

A. Have the students open their Bibles. Read Romans 8:38–39 and Song of Song 2:4 with them.

B. Begin a dialog by asking them to give their thoughts about the messages conveyed in these verses about God's character.

C. Have your students identify three truths about the constancy of God's love based on these verses.

- Truth #1:

- Truth #2:

- Truth #3:

D. Have your students identify the three most important points in each passage.

Romans 8:38–39

- Attribute #1:

- Attribute #2:

- Attribute #3:

Song of Solomon 2:4

- Attribute #1:

- Attribute #2

- Attribute #3:

PART THREE: The Application

In this section, you will help the students identify areas of their lives where they can apply God's Word and experience His emotions.

Note: They should have their journals with them and be prepared to write in them.

A. Ask the students to identify and write in their journals the emotions they have knowing they are His Bride and His Beloved.

B. Ask the students to journal the thoughts they have about knowing that in the midst of temptation and past failure there is still a banner of love over them that cannot be removed.

C. Ask the students to identify and write in their journals the areas in their lives that are obstacles, though they may seem ok, good, or even fun.

D. Explain to your students that sometimes God speaks to us about how much He loves other people. Ask them to journal any visions, dreams, or words that others have spoken over them about God's destiny and heart for them.

E. Ask the students to write down their feelings about the truth that nothing created is able to separate them from the love of Christ.

F. Ask the students to consider how a relationship with God is meant to sustain and comfort them and help them overcome difficulties and struggles.

PART FOUR: The Impact

    A. Play the song again. Give a copy of the lyrics to each student, and ask them to sing along.

    B. Lead your students in prayer by waiting on the Lord and being silent before Him.

    C. Ask the students to pray one at a time a prayer of thanksgiving for the death and resurrection of Christ.

    D. Ask the students one at a time to pray for those who they know are separated from the love of God by not being in relationship with Christ.

    E. Print the following prayer, and give a copy to each student. Pray it together out loud.

Thank you, God, for sending Your only Son to die for my sins. Thank you for doing it because You love me, and You won't let anything come between us in love. Thank you that Jesus' death and resurrection make it possible for me to have victory over things in my life that would keep me from You. Help me to put all of my trust in His cross and in the power of the Holy Spirit.

Thank you, God, that You have made the church a Bride for Your Son. Help me to understand what it means to be under Your banner of love.

I close the door to areas in my life where Satan has had a grip. I ask, God, that You would give me strength to put all my trust in You. Fill me with the Holy Spirit and the power that is in the cross of Christ. In Jesus' name, amen.

    F. Invite the Holy Spirit to visit your students, and ask if there is anyone who would like individual prayer. Pray for them, and ask others to join you in praying for them when appropriate.

Prayer

Student Journal and Notes

_____

_____

_____

_____

_____

_____

_____

_____

_____

_____

_____

_____

_____

_____

LESSON FOUR: One Thing

Biblical Foundation: "One Thing"
Song: "Dance With Me"

Objective: To help the students understand that there is much more to this life than we often think. David asked the Lord for the one thing that matters the most. Through Jesus, we can boldly approach the throne room of God and dwell in His presence, and this is that one thing. His love is better than life, better than anything we might experience in this world. This lesson will explore Psalm 27:4 and what it means to dwell in the house of the Lord and behold His beauty.

Resource Materials Needed:

- *Prayer* CD
- Sound system to play the CD
- Handouts of the lyrics to "Dance With Me"
- Your Bible and a Bible for each student
- Your journal and a journal for each student
- Handouts of the Apostolic Prayers

I.   The Invitation: Into the Heart of God

This step will assist you in preparing to bring the heart of the message together with the heart of the music, while embracing God's heart for the students you will be teaching.

A. Listen to "Dance With Me" several times.

B. As you listen to the song, write in your journal the key phrases and lyrics that impact you the most.

C. Reflect on the truth that He desires to bring you to the place where you desire to dwell in His presence and seek to gaze on His beauty.

D. Reflect on your personal prayer time. What are some of the things that get in the way of your having time with God?

II. The Impartation: Into the Knowledge of God

This step will help you understand why the song was written and identify the main points to communicate from it. It will also help you gain insight into the biblical foundations of the lesson and the song as you consider the truths contained in each.

A. Main points to the song "Dance With Me"

1. This song was incorporated in this theme because of its message regarding the unchanging nature of God's love. All else will fade away when Jesus makes everything new, but His love is constant and will remain forever.

2. This song encourages us to reflect on both God's glory and the love that He sings over us. The lyrics speak of the refreshment and pleasure that are the result of spending time with Him.

3. "Dance With Me" is a cry for authenticity in our walk with God, to truly have a close relationship with Him and not just talk about Him as someone who is far away.

4. The desire to know God and understand His ways causes us to press into Him. This song inspires us to lay down all of the pleasures of this life in pursuit of that one thing—to see His beauty and be with Him where He is.

B. Biblical Foundation: Read, study, and meditate on Psalm 27:4.

One thing I have desired of the Lord, that I will seek: That I may dwell in the house of the Lord all the days of my life, to behold the beauty of the Lord, and to inquire in His temple.

Key Points to Remember

1 This Psalm demonstrates David's chief desire to worship and wait on the Lord.

2. The text of the Psalm in its entirety reveals David's devotion to God's house.

3. In his commentary on Psalm 27:4, Charles Spurgeon points out that "divided aims tend to distraction, weakness, disappointment."[1] When we look at this verse in context, we see that it was in the house of the Lord that David found his purpose and strength.

4. The desires of our heart are important to God. He desires to give us the good desires along with Himself, but He will also judge us according to our evil desires (Psalm 145; Romans 1:18–32).

5. An important lesson to learn from David is that gazing on the Lord and dwelling in His house can and should be our first desire no matter what our situation may be. Spurgeon states that "under David's painful circumstances we might have expected him to desire repose, safety, and a thousand other good things, but no, he has set his heart on the pearl, and leaves the rest."

6. As Spurgeon says, "holy desires must lead to resolute action." If we truly desire God, we will actively seek Him by reading the Bible, worshipping and giving ourselves to prayer.

7. It may sound odd or at least difficult to gaze on God when we can't see Him. Beholding God is simply getting to know Him better through prayer and study. Meditating on the wonders of God and who He is as the Father, Son, and Holy Spirit is seeing that He is beautiful and it makes us love Him more.

---

1   Spurgeon, Charles H. "Psalm 27." The Treasury of David. http://www.spurgeon.org/treasury/ps027.htm.

III. Preparation: Action Plan and Lesson Presentation Template

This step will help you develop an action plan to communicate the lesson using a template. This presentation template has been designed to assist you in organizing and presenting the material in the most effective manner.

Bear in mind all that you have considered and learned by contemplating the song and studying the lesson.

We, as teachers, are to serve our students; they are not to serve us. Remember that we do so in order that they may in turn serve God with a greater understanding of His ways in their lives. Be sensitive to the needs of the students, keeping in mind that God is faithful and good and knows them best.

"S.E.R.V.A.N.T." spelled out is:

S: "Share"—Share your life with your students.

E: "Example"—Be an example of the truth to them.

R: "Represent"—Represent Christ correctly to your students.

V: "Voice"—Help them learn to recognize God's voice.

A: "Authority"—Teach in the power of God with His authority.

N: "Needs"—Meet the needs of your students so that God is glorified.

T: "Train and Teach"—As you train and teach, do so rightly dividing the Word of God.

Lesson Presentation Template

Theme: Prayer

Lesson: "One Thing"

Lesson Biblical Foundation: Psalm 27:4

Song: "Dance With Me"

PART ONE: The Invitation

In this section, you will invite your students to know your heart for them to embrace the lesson you are teaching. Be transparent and reachable. Communicate your desire for them to experience from the lesson the heart and love God has for them.

A. Play "Dance With Me" several times.

B. Have your students mediate on the beauty of the Lord. A sample question to help give them direction is "What makes God beautiful?" It may also be helpful to explain meditation as clearing away all the clutter in their minds and hearts to focus on God.

C. Share with your students your responses to the following questions.

a. Have there been times in your life when you felt so close to God that nothing else mattered? How would you describe that feeling?

b. How has studying Psalm 27:4 impacted you?

c. Do you think you will make any changes in your life as a result of studying this lesson? What practical things will you do in your pursuit of the one thing?

d. Spend a few minutes sharing about the heart God has given you for your students. Choose a portion of Scripture from the Apostolic Prayers handout, and pray it over them.

PART TWO: The Impartation

In this section, you will invite the students into the knowledge of God through His Word.

A. Have the students open their Bibles, and read Psalm 27:4 with them.

B. Begin a dialog by asking them to identify David's goals in this verse and share their thoughts about why this was so important to him.

C. Ask your students what they think David meant when he asked to dwell in the house of the Lord.

D. Identify with the students how David in the midst of his struggles and wars with the flesh and people, could cry out to God to never be separated from His house. Discuss how David sought the dwelling place of God even during difficult times. Ask them why they think it's important to pray and read the Bible in the midst of conflict and struggle.

E. Have your students identify at least three things David knew about God that made him want to dwell in His house.

- #1

- #2

- #3

F. Ask your students to list three things that they think are beautiful.

- #1

- #2

- #3

G. Have them make another list of at least three reasons they think God is even more beautiful.

- #1

- #2

- #3

PART THREE: The Application

In this section, you will help the students identify areas of their lives where they can apply God's Word and experience His emotions.

Note: They should have their journals with them and be prepared to write in them.

A. Give some examples of distractions, those things that can waste time and make us feel bored with God. Explain how these things can cause false love to divert their attention from the reality of God. Ask them to write down things that could be distracting them personally. Lead them in a corporate prayer, asking the Holy Spirit to give them a desire to seek God with all their heart.

B. Point out that when we seek to dwell in the house of the Lord, His word becomes more alive to us. Ask them to journal their thoughts related to this.

C. Talk about God's desire to fascinate us. Tell your students about how He wants us to be excited about prayer. Have them identify two relationships in their lives that can challenge them to stay hungry and thirsty for the things of God (for example, their parents or pastor).

Prayer

PART FOUR: The Impact

A. Play the song again. Give a copy of the lyrics to each student and ask them to sing along.

B. Lead your students in prayer by waiting on the Lord and being silent before Him.

C. Have the students write out a prayer, thanking God for all that He has done for them.

D. Ask the students to pray one at a time for God's Word to come alive in their hearts and lives.

E. Ask the students to pray one at a time for those who they know are separated from the love of God by not being in relationship with Christ.

F. Print the following prayer, and give a copy to each student. Pray it together out loud.

Thank you, God, for sending Your only Son to die for my sins. Thank you for revealing Your love and gladness through Jesus.

I close the door to the areas in my life where Satan has had a grip. I ask, God, that You would give me strength to put all of my trust in You. Fill me with the Holy Spirit and the power that is in the cross of Christ.

God, help me understand what it means to dwell in Your house. Show me how to gaze on Your beauty. I want to see You better so that I can love You better. In Jesus' name, amen.

G. Invite the Holy Spirit to visit your students, and ask if there is anyone who would like individual prayer. Pray for them, and ask others to join you in praying for them when appropriate.

Student Journal and Notes

LESSON FIVE: Thy Kingdom Come

Biblical Foundation: Matthew 6:9–13
Song: "The Lord's Prayer"

Objective: To take a closer look at the Lord's Prayer. What did Jesus tell us to pray for and why did He emphasize those things? How does being familiar with this prayer affect the way we pray every day?

Resource Materials Needed:

- *Prayer* CD
- Sound system to play the CD
- Handouts of the lyrics to "The Lord's Prayer"
- Your Bible and a Bible for each student
- Your journal and a journal for each student
- Handouts of the Apostolic Prayers

Prayer

I. The Invitation: Into the Heart of God

This step will assist you in preparing to bring the heart of the message together with the heart of the music, while embracing God's heart for the students you will be teaching.

A. Listen to "The Lord's Prayer" several times.

B. As you listen to the song, write in your journal the key phrases and lyrics that impact you the most.

C. Reflect on each of the points that Jesus focused on in His prayer. Journal your thoughts on the meaning and implications of each statement:

    a. "… hallowed be Your name."

    b. "Your kingdom come. Your will be done…"

    c. "Give us … our daily bread."

    d. "Forgive us … as we forgive our debtors."

II. The Impartation: Into the Knowledge of God

This step will help you understand why the song was written and identify the main points to communicate from it. It will also help you gain insight into the biblical foundations of the lesson and the song as you consider the truths contained in each.

A. Main points to the song "The Lord's Prayer"

1. This song was composed and arranged in such a way as to help children connect with Jesus' desire for us to pray.

2. This prayer being sung by children encourages us to reflect on God as a Father, His Will and His Kingdom coming to earth, Jesus as our daily bread, and the great need we have to be forgiven and to forgive. There are no additional lyrics in the song other than the Lord's Prayer so that we can focus on the importance of Jesus' words.

B. Biblical Foundation: Read, study, and meditate on Matthew 6:9–13.

In this manner, therefore, pray: our Father in heaven, hallowed be Your name. Your kingdom come. Your will be done on earth as it is in heaven. Give us this day our daily bread. And forgive us our debts, as we forgive our debtors. And do not lead us into temptation, but deliver us from the evil one. For Yours is the kingdom and the power and the glory forever. Amen.

Key Points to Remember

1. *"Our Father in heaven"*: The opening phrase sets the tone for the rest of the prayer, addressing God as our heavenly Father. Beginning in this way fixes our hearts and minds on the fact that we are talking to the One who is more loving and kind than all others. Knowing that He is like this builds up our confidence to ask Him for things.

2. *"Hallowed be Your name"*: Even though we come before a gracious and compassionate God, He is still holy, and there is no one like Him. He is to be feared. We need to remember this in order to avoid over-familiarity with Him and maintain the appropriate respect and admiration that He is due.

3. *"Your kingdom come. Your will be done..."*: The word "kingdom" here refers to the power and authority of God, His right to rule and reign. His Kingdom is far more than just a territory or nation. He will have rightful control of everything in Heaven and on Earth. It is important for us to acknowledge that He is our leader and that His leadership is perfect.

4. *"Give us ... our daily bread"*: We know that God alone provides everything we need both physically and spiritually. During Jesus' time of temptation in the wilderness (Matthew 4), He encouraged Himself with the knowledge that "man shall not live by bread alone; but ... by every word that proceeds from the mouth of the LORD" (Deuteronomy 8:3). This petition implies our dependence on God for the supply of our needs.

5. *"Forgive us ... as we forgive our debtors"*: Most translations use the words "debts" and "debtors." It is the same language that Paul uses in Colossians 2 when he speaks of Christ's victory over our sin—it is our forgiveness and freedom. He paid the ransom price that we could not and canceled the sin of debt that we owed to God. The only debt we now owe is one of love.

6. *"And do not lead us into temptation, but deliver us from evil"*: Psalm 141:4 is a similar prayer: "Do not incline my heart to any evil thing, to practice wicked works with men who do iniquity..." It is important for us to understand that God Himself does not tempt us (James 1:13), and He alone can help us resist temptation and choose righteousness.

III. Preparation: Action Plan and Lesson Presentation Template

This step will help you develop an action plan to communicate the lesson using a template. This presentation template has been designed to assist you in organizing and presenting the material in the most effective manner.

Bear in mind all that you have considered and learned by contemplating the song and studying the lesson.

We, as teachers, are to serve our students; they are not to serve us. Remember that we do so in order that they may in turn serve God with a greater understanding of His ways in their lives. Be sensitive to the needs of the students, keeping in mind that God is faithful and good and knows them best.

"S.E.R.V.A.N.T." spelled out is:

S: "Share"—Share your life with your students.

E: "Example"—Be an example of the truth to them.

R: "Represent"—Represent Christ correctly to your students.

V: "Voice"—Help them learn to recognize God's voice.

A: "Authority"—Teach in the power of God with His authority.

N: "Needs"—Meet the needs of your students so that God is glorified.

T: "Train and Teach"—As you train and teach, do so rightly dividing the Word of God.

Lesson Presentation Template

Theme: Prayer

Lesson: "The Lord's Prayer"

Lesson Biblical Foundation: Matthew 6:9–13

Song: "The Lord's Prayer"

PART ONE: The Invitation

In this section, you will invite your students to know your heart for them to embrace the lesson you are teaching. Be transparent and reachable. Communicate your desire for them to experience from the lesson the heart and love God has for them.

A. Play "The Lord's Prayer" several times.

B. Have your students mediate on it for a few minutes.

C. Share with your students your responses to the following questions.

    a. What have you been praying for lately?

    b. How has studying the Lord's Prayer affected the way you view prayer?

    c. Do you think you will pray differently now? How so?

    d. Spend a few minutes sharing about the heart God has given you for your students. Choose a portion of Scripture from the Apostolic Prayers handout and pray it over them.

PART TWO: The Impartation

In this section, you will invite the students into the knowledge of God through His Word.

    A. Have the students open their Bibles. Read Matthew 6:9–13 with them.

    B. Begin a dialog by asking them to identify the key phrases (see Part II above). Then discuss what they think each phrase means.

Prayer

PART THREE: The Application

In this section, you will help the students identify areas of their lives where they can apply God's Word and experience His emotions.

Note: They should have their journals with them and be prepared to write in them.

    A. Ask the students to write in their journals the key phrases that they just discussed.

    B. Have each student write a paraphrase of the Lord's Prayer. This will help them see how it applies to the Church as a whole, but also to each of them individually.

PART FOUR: The Impact

A. Play the song again. Give a copy of the lyrics to each student, and ask them to sing along.

B. Print the following prayer, and give a copy to each student. Pray it together out loud.

Thank you, God, for sending Your only Son to die for my sins. Thank you for all of the things that Jesus taught us while He was on Earth. Thank you that He taught us how to pray.

I pray that You will not lead me into temptation, but will deliver me from evil. And I close the door to the areas in my life where Satan has had a grip. I ask, God, that through the power of the Holy Spirit, You would give me strength to put all my concerns, hurts and trials into Your hands and trust Jesus as my Savior and Lord.

God, I want to learn how to pray so that I can touch Your heart and have You touch mine. In Jesus' name, amen.

C. Invite the Holy Spirit to visit your students, and ask if there is anyone who would like individual prayer. Pray for them, and ask others to join you in praying for them when appropriate.

Prayer

Student Journal and Notes

LESSON SIX: God's Goodness Sustains Our Hearts

Biblical Foundation: Deuteronomy 31:6, Hebrews 13:5, 1 Peter 5:7, Proverbs 18:24
Song: "So Good to Me"

Objective: This lesson is designed to explore the faithfulness and goodness of God as our friend, the One who sticks closer than a brother. God knows everything that is happening in our lives and really cares for us. When we grasp the truth that He will never leave us nor forsake us, that He is wholly trustworthy, our hearts are filled with the courage to follow Him.

Resource Materials Needed:

- *Prayer* CD
- Sound system to play the CD
- Handouts of the lyrics to "So Good To Me"
- Your Bible and a Bible for each student
- Your journal and a journal for each student
- Handouts of the Apostolic Prayers

I.   The Invitation: Into the Heart of God

This step will assist you in preparing to bring the heart of the message together with the heart of the music, while embracing God's heart for the students you will be teaching.

A. Listen to "So Good to Me" several times.

B. As you listen to the song, write in your journal the key phrases and lyrics from the song that impact you the most.

C. Reflect on the times you have seen how God cares for you. How have you seen Him hold your life in His hands and stay by your side? Examples of this could be comfort and encouragement or provision.

D. Reflect on how we are not living only for our lives on Earth, but we are living for an eternity of fellowship with the One who created us and loved us since the beginning of time.

II. The Impartation: Into the Knowledge of God

This step will help you understand why the song was written and identify the main points to communicate from it. It will also help you gain insight into the biblical foundations of the lesson and the song as you consider the truths contained in each.

A. Main points to the song "So Good To Me"

1. The overarching message in this song is the goodness of God. He expresses it to us through His faithfulness. He will never leave nor forsake us.

2. Words like "I see the love you have in your eyes," and "I hear the song that you sing over me" reveal how God sustains our hearts and speaks life to our spirits.

3. Some people find it difficult to fully trust God in certain situations, and this causes them to harden their hearts just enough to keep them from recognizing or experiencing His goodness. This song endeavors to communicate that God is completely trustworthy no matter where we go, no matter what we do.

B. Biblical Foundation: Read, study, and meditate on Deuteronomy 31:6, Hebrews 13:5, 1 Peter 5:7, Proverbs 18:24

Be strong and of good courage, do not fear nor be afraid of them; for the Lord your God, He is the One who goes with you. He will not leave you nor forsake you. (Deuteronomy 31:6)

Let your conduct be without covetousness; be content with such things as you have. For He Himself has said, "I will never leave you nor forsake you." (Hebrews 13:5)

Key Points to Remember

1. We are often unsatisfied with what we have when we see what others have, but God calls us to be content with what He has given us. This can mean possessions or position. He knows us and our needs even better than we do.

2. God has promised to neither leave nor forsake us. Believing this promise and being secure in His love will help us find confidence in our relationships with other people.

3. Life is full of unknowns—things like moving to a new town or going to a new school—and this can be unsettling. But God has promised to go with us and walk alongside us.

…Casting all your care upon Him, for He cares for you. (1 Peter 5:7)

Key Points to Remember

1. Sometimes, being humble in all of our relationships is a difficult thing to do. But God has told us that we should cast all of our cares upon Him, because no one cares for us as much as He does. This certainly includes anxiety caused by people misunderstanding and mistreating us.

2. When we are mistreated, it is the natural response to become defensive, but God has told us to be humble and pray for those who persecute us.

A man who has friends must himself be friendly, but there is a friend who sticks closer than a brother. (Proverbs 18:24)

Key Points to Remember

1. Jesus did not simply give us the best example of friendship; He demonstrated the only true friendship there is: a love that pours out its very life.

2. We develop close relationships by serving those we love. The way we extend friendship to others should be with humility and love.

III. Preparation: Action Plan and Lesson Presentation Template

This step will help you develop an action plan to communicate the lesson using a template. This presentation template has been designed to assist you in organizing and presenting the material in the most effective manner.

Bear in mind all that you have considered and learned by contemplating the song and studying the lesson.

We, as teachers, are to serve our students; they are not to serve us. Remember that we do so in order that they may in turn serve God with a greater understanding of His ways in their lives. Be sensitive to the needs of the students, keeping in mind that God is faithful and good and knows them best.

"S.E.R.V.A.N.T." spelled out is:

S: "Share"—Share your life with your students.

E: "Example"—Be an example of the truth to them.

R: "Represent"—Represent Christ correctly to your students.

V: "Voice"—Help them learn to recognize God's voice.

A: "Authority"—Teach in the power of God with His authority.

N: "Needs"—Meet the needs of your students so that God is glorified.

T: "Train and Teach"—As you train and teach, do so rightly dividing the Word of God.

Prayer

Lesson Presentation Template

Theme: Prayer

Lesson: "God's Goodness Sustains Our Hearts"

Lesson Biblical Foundation: Deuteronomy 31:6, Hebrews 13:5, 1 Peter 5:7, Proverbs 18:24

Song: "So Good to Me"

PART ONE: The Invitation

In this section, you will invite your students to know your heart for them to embrace the lesson you are teaching. Be transparent and reachable. Communicate your desire for them to experience from the lesson the heart and love God has for them.

A. Play "So Good to Me" several times.

B. Ask the students to mediate on the goodness of the Lord in their lives as they listen to the lyrics.

C. Share with your students your responses to the following questions.

   a. How has studying and reflecting on the verses in this lesson impacted your understanding of God's goodness?

   b. When in your life have you seen God's goodness the most?

   c. Do you relate to God's goodness as a part of His unchanging character, or just attribute it to circumstances?

   d. How much freedom do you have to be honest with the Lord about your feelings?

   e. How do you define friendship? How do you think God defines it?

   f. Spend a few minutes sharing about the heart God has given you for your students. Choose a portion of Scripture from the Apostolic Prayers handout and pray it over them.

PART TWO: The Impartation

In this section, you will invite the students into the knowledge of God through His Word.

    A. Have the students open their Bibles. Read the foundational verses with them.

        1. Read Deuteronomy 31:6 and Hebrews 13:5 together. Ask your students about some of the things they're afraid of. How can God help them be brave?

        2. Have the students read 1 Peter 5:7. Discuss with your students God's concern for us, that He sees and knows and cares about what is going on in our lives. Ask them to think of three things they know about God that show how much He cares.

            • #1

            • #2

            • #3

        3. Read Proverbs 18:24 with your students. Invite your students to share about friendship. Ask them to tell you what they think it means to be a good friend. Discuss what it means to have friendship with God.

PART THREE: The Application

In this section, you will help the students identify areas of their lives where they can apply God's Word and experience His emotions.

Note: They should have their journals with them and be prepared to write in them.

    A. Share with your students about some hard times you have faced and how God helped you through them. Then, have them journal about some of their own experiences.

    B. Ask the students to journal about times when they didn't trust in the Lord. How did they feel? What did they think? Will they trust Him more now, and in what circumstances?

PART FOUR: The Impact

A. Play the song again. Give a copy of the lyrics to each student and ask them to sing along.

B. Lead your students in prayer by waiting on the Lord and being silent before Him.

C. Have the students write out a prayer to thank God for all that He has done for them.

D. Ask the students to pray one at a time for God's Word to come alive in their hearts and lives.

E. Ask them to pray one at a time for those who they know are going through a difficult time. (You may want to give some examples.)

F. Have them read aloud the lyrics to "So Good to Me" as a prayer.

G. Print the following prayer, and give a copy to each student. Pray it together out loud.

Thank you, God, for sending Your only Son to die for my sins. Thank you that You are not just my teacher or master, but You are my friend.

I close the door to the areas in my life where Satan has had a grip. I ask, God, that through the power of the Holy Spirit, You would give me strength to put all my trust into Your hands and fill me with the Holy Spirit and the power that is in the cross of Christ.

Help me to recognize Your goodness and to remember Your faithfulness for all my life. Thank you for Your promise to never leave or forsake me. In Jesus' name, amen.

H. Invite the Holy Spirit to visit your students, and ask if there is anyone who would like individual prayer. Pray for them, and ask others to join you in praying for them when appropriate.

Prayer

Student Journal and Notes

_____

_____

_____

_____

_____

_____

_____

_____

_____

_____

_____

_____

_____

_____

LESSON SEVEN: His Name Is Great Among All the Nations

Biblical Foundation: Malachi 1:11
Song: "Wide, Wide World"

Objective: This lesson will reveal that when we declare with our mouths the truth of who God is, we come into alignment with His Word and destroy accusations against Him that may exist in our hearts.

Resource Materials Needed:

- *Prayer* CD
- Sound system to play the CD
- Handouts of the lyrics to "Wide, Wide World"
- Your Bible and a Bible for each student
- Your journal and a journal for each student
- Handouts of the Apostolic Prayers

Prayer

I.   The Invitation: Into the Heart of God

This step will assist you in preparing to bring the heart of the message together with the heart of the music, while embracing God's heart for the students you will be teaching.

A. Listen to "Wide, Wide World" several times.

B. Think about the greatness of His love for all of creation, especially for people.

C. As you listen to the song, reflect on God's strength in your life. Write in your journal your thoughts and feelings about the reality that all the earth shall praise Him.

D. Meditate on why He will receive such praise. What makes Him so worthy (love, strength, etc.)? Use Psalms 47:1–2 and 148:13 as well.

E. Consider those things that hinder you from praising God with all your heart. What are some practical things you can do to remove those hindrances?

II. The Impartation: Into the Knowledge of God

This step will help you understand why the song was written and identify the main points to communicate from it. It will also help you gain insight into the biblical foundations of the lesson and the song as you consider the truths contained in each.

A. Main points to the song "Wide, Wide World"

1. This song reveals how we can encounter the heart of God and be filled with praise for His name. It reminds us that it is right for all creation to praise Him.

2. The first prayer in this song reminds us of God's faithfulness to defeat our enemies when we lift our voices in praise (Psalm 8:2).

3. Sometimes we need to remind ourselves to praise God—to dance, sing and shout. He is always worthy of our worship no matter how we feel or what our circumstances may be.

B. Biblical Foundation: Read, study and meditate on Malachi 1:11.

"...From the rising of the sun, even to its going down, My name shall be great among the Gentiles; in every place, incense shall be offered to My name and a pure offering; for My name shall be great among the nations," says the Lord of hosts.

Key Points to Remember

1. When the Jews returned from the Babylonian exile, they rebuilt the temple and had high hopes of reestablishing their city and culture.

2. Unfortunately, they found that this was harder than they expected. They suffered from drought, famine and almost constant enemy attacks; before long, Judah began to doubt the loving faithfulness of God. Their doubt turned into blame and accusation against Him, which negatively affected their hearts in worship.

3. The wicked seemed to prosper while the righteous struggled. Therefore, they became careless in following God's commandments because there didn't seem to be any benefit to faithful obedience. They brought injured, crippled or diseased animals to offer as sacrifices to God instead of bringing their very best. They were not wholehearted in worship.

4. Malachi spoke to Judah about these sins and called them to repentance, to return to the Lord and purify their worship. He reminded them of the wisdom of the fear of the Lord—that they should put their trust in Him rather than a form of godliness in keeping the Law, but not with their whole hearts. He wanted the people to understand that if they would repent, purify their worship, and obey the Law, God's blessing would surely come (3:10).

5. God declares Himself to be the Lord that does not change (3:6). His love is holy and unchanging, and He keeps every promise. The great day of the Lord will come when He will punish the wicked and vindicate the righteous. This day will be preceded by the spirit of Elijah, which will turn the hearts of the fathers and children (4:5–6).

III. Preparation: Action Plan and Lesson Presentation Template

This step will help you develop an action plan to communicate the lesson using a template. This presentation template has been designed to assist you in organizing and presenting the material in the most effective manner.

Bear in mind all that you have considered and learned by contemplating the song and studying the lesson.

We, as teachers, are to serve our students; they are not to serve us. Remember that we do so in order that they may in turn serve God with a greater understanding of His ways in their lives. Be sensitive to the needs of the students, keeping in mind that God is faithful and good and knows them best.

"S.E.R.V.A.N.T." spelled out is:

S: "Share"—Share your life with your students.

E: "Example"—Be an example of the truth to them.

R: "Represent"—Represent Christ correctly to your students.

V: "Voice"—Help them learn to recognize God's voice.

A: "Authority"—Teach in the power of God with His authority.

N: "Needs"—Meet the needs of your students so that God is glorified.

T: "Train and Teach"—As you train and teach, do so rightly dividing the Word of God.

Prayer

Lesson Presentation Template

Theme: Prayer

Lesson: "His Name is Great Among All the Nations"

Lesson Biblical Foundation: Malachi 1:11

Song: "Wide, Wide World"

PART ONE: The Invitation

In this section, you will invite your students to know your heart for them to embrace the lesson you are teaching. Be transparent and reachable. Communicate your desire for them to experience from the lesson the heart and love God has for them.

A. Play "Wide, Wide World" several times.

B. Using the song and the Scripture as a starting point, mediate on the greatness of God and how worthy He is to be praised. It may be helpful to explain meditation as clearing away all the clutter in their minds and hearts to focus on God.

C. Share with your students your responses to the following questions.

   a. What do you think it means to praise God? Is it just singing songs, or are there other ways to praise Him?

   b. What do you think it will look like when all the nations acknowledge the greatness of God?

   c. How has studying Malachi 1:11 affected the way you think of pure worship?

   d. What changes do you plan to make in regard to the way you present yourself to God in worship?

   e. Spend a few minutes sharing about the heart God has given you for your students. Choose a portion of Scripture from the Apostolic Prayers handout, and pray it over them.

PART TWO: The Impartation

In this section, you will invite the students into the knowledge of God through His Word.

A. Have the students open their Bibles. Read Malachi 1:6–14 with them.

B. Share with them the historical context of the book. Talk about what Malachi was probably feeling when he prophesied to Israel.

C. Ask the students to think about ways that we blame bad situations on God and how this makes our hearts hard toward Him.

D. Discuss with them how we sometimes compare what we have with what someone else has who doesn't love God. When we do this, we are not trusting in God's goodness to provide everything we need when we seek first His righteousness.

E. From the passages, identify at least three attributes of God that reveal His faithfulness to us. How do these attributes assure us that He will not bless the wicked, and how sin can hinder and prevent us from serving Him and from having fellowship with Him?

- #1

- #2

- #3

PART THREE: The Application

In this section, you will help the students identify areas of their lives where they can apply God's Word and experience His emotions.

Note: They should have their journals with them and be prepared to write in them.

A. Ask the students to identify things that distract them during worship. Give them some suggestions for ways that they can engage themselves in corporate worship.

B. Communicate to your students God's desire that we have our hearts free to pray, sing and dance, and challenge them to stay hungry and thirsty for the things of God. Discuss how praise and the Word of God help us to enjoy prayer because they help us recognize lies about God. Ask your students to identify accusations against God that are not true, but that they have believed. Have them write down what they know is true about God next to the accusation.

C. Give them a moment to reflect on God's desire to encounter them in worship and prayer. Talk about how they can be free to pray, sing and dance for the Lord. Then, lead them in a corporate prayer, asking the Lord to help them enter into pure worship and have freedom in prayer to be honest with God about their feelings.

D. Ask the students to journal what they think it will be like when the whole earth praises God.

PART FOUR: The Impact

A. Play the song again. Give a copy of the lyrics to each student, and ask them to sing along.

B. Lead your students in prayer by waiting on the Lord and being silent before Him. Ask the students one at a time to pray for those who they know are separated from the love of God by not being in relationship with Christ.

C. Ask the students to pray one at a time for God's Word to come alive in their heart and lives. Have them meditate on the cross of Christ and the blood of Jesus that was shed for their sins.

D. Have the students write out a prayer acknowledging God for all that He has revealed to them through this lesson. (For example, His goodness and faithfulness when we pursue His Kingdom.)

E. Print the following prayer and give a copy to each student. Pray it together out loud.

Thank you, God, for sending Your only Son to die for my sins so that I can be with You forever.

Help me remember to praise Your name at all times, no matter what. I want to follow Your ways and trust You to give me what I need. I close the door to the areas in my life where Satan has had a grip. I ask, God, that through the power of the Holy Spirit, You would give me strength to put all my trust into Your hands and fill me with the Holy Spirit and the power that is in the cross of Christ.

Fill me with the knowledge that Your Son is returning for me with love in His heart. In Jesus' name, amen.

F. Invite the Holy Spirit to visit your students and ask if there is anyone who would like individual prayer. Pray for them and ask others to join you in praying for them when appropriate.

Prayer

Student Journal and Notes

_____

_____

_____

_____

_____

_____

_____

_____

_____

_____

_____

_____

_____

_____

LESSON EIGHT: Who is Like You, O God?
A Review of Past Lessons

Biblical Foundation: Psalm 71:19
Song: "Eden Elysium"

Objective: This lesson looks back at what was covered in the first seven lessons.

Resource Materials Needed:

- *Prayer* CD
- Sound system to play the CD
- Your Bible and a Bible for each student
- Your journal and a journal for each student
- Handouts of the Apostolic Prayers

Prayer

I.   The Invitation: Into the Heart of God

This step will assist you in preparing to bring the heart of the message together with the heart of the music, while embracing the heart of God for the students you will be teaching.

   A. Listen to "Eden Elysium" several times. Engage with the prayers that the children are praying.

   B. Pray for each of your students to receive a desire to pray. Ask the Holy Spirit to help them see that prayer is more than just routine words.

   C. Read Psalm 71:19 as you listen to the song. Journal your thoughts on how you can hear this declaration coming through the prayers of the children.

II. The Impartation: Into the Knowledge of God

This step will help you understand why the song was written and identify the main points to communicate from it. It will also help you gain insight into the biblical foundations of the lesson and the song as you consider the truths contained in each.

    A. Main points to the song "Eden Elysium"

        1. This song contains mighty prayers of faith and hope from children.

        2. It is intended to move us to reflect on the thought that there is no one like God.

        3. The prayers of the children in this song are meant to encourage us to pray for the students we lead and teach.

        4. "Eden Elysium" is intended to impart a vision to us, one of seeing this generation be glad to enter into the place of prayer.

    B. Biblical Foundation: Read, study, and meditate on Psalm 71:19.

        Also, Your righteousness, O God, is very high, You who have done great things; O God, who is like You?

    C. Read, review and meditate on the verses and passages referred to in the past seven lessons.

    D. Write Down Key Points from Each Lesson

        1. Letting God Unlock Our Hearts—Zephaniah 3:17; Psalm 139:17–18

        2. We Are Known By God—Ephesians 1:3–6

        3. God's Glad Heart—Romans 8:38–39; Song of Solomon 2:4

        4. One Thing—Psalm 27:4

        5. Thy Kingdom Come—Matthew 6:9–13

Prayer

6. God's Goodness Sustains Our Hearts—Deuteronomy 31:6; Hebrews 13:5; 1 Peter 5:7; Proverbs 18:24

7. His Name Is Great Among All the Nations—Malachi 1:11

III. Preparation: Action Plan and Lesson Presentation Template

This step will help you develop an action plan to communicate the lesson using a template. This presentation template has been designed to assist you in organizing and presenting the material in the most effective manner.

Bear in mind all that you have considered and learned by contemplating the song and studying the lesson.

We, as teachers, are to serve our students; they are not to serve us. Remember that we do so in order that they may in turn serve God with a greater understanding of His ways in their lives. Be sensitive to the needs of the students, keeping in mind that God is faithful and good and knows them best.

"S.E.R.V.A.N.T." spelled out is:

S: "Share"—Share your life with your students.

E: "Example"—Be an example of the truth to them.

R: "Represent"—Represent Christ correctly to your students.

V: "Voice"—Help them learn to recognize God's voice.

A: "Authority"—Teach in the power of God with His authority.

N: "Needs"—Meet the needs of your students so that God is glorified.

T: "Train and Teach"—As you train and teach, do so rightly dividing the Word of God.

Lesson Presentation Template

Theme: Prayer

Lesson: "Who is Like You, O God?"

Lesson Biblical Foundation: Psalm 71:19

Song: "Eden Elysium"

PART ONE: The Invitation

In this section, you will invite your students to know your heart for them to embrace the lesson you are teaching. Be transparent and reachable. Communicate your desire for them to experience from the lesson the heart and love God has for them.

A. Play "Eden Elysium" several times. Encourage your students to engage with the prayers of the children on the CD.

B. Share with your students those things that have impacted you from past lessons.

   a. What have you learned from studying the scriptures in the past lessons? How has that changed the way you pray? Give some specific examples.

   b. Talk about your relationship with God. How does that affect your desire to give yourself to prayer?

   c. Spend a few minutes sharing with your students about your heart for them to pray and dialogue with God.

   d. Spend a few minutes sharing about the heart God has given you for your students. Choose a portion of Scripture from the Apostolic Prayers handout and pray it over them.

PART TWO: The Impartation

In this section, you will invite the students into the knowledge of God through His Word.

A. Share with your students that the previous lessons were designed to show them that there is no one like God.

B. Have them open their Bibles and read all of the Scriptures referenced in the past lessons.

C. Discuss with the students how prayer helps us understand who God is. Talk about how knowing Him better changes the way we pray.

PART THREE: The Application and Impact

In this section, you will help the students identify areas of their lives where they can apply God's Word and experience His emotions.

Note: They should have their journals with them and be prepared to write in them.

  A. Play "Eden Elysium" again and have the children meditate on the prayers. Ask them to journal their thoughts and what God speaks to them.

  B. Lead the students in a time of prayer. Begin by waiting on the Lord.

  C. Have the students write out a prayer to thank God for all that He has revealed to them through this lesson.

  D. Print the following prayer and give a copy to each student. Pray it together out loud.

Thank you, God, for sending Your only Son to die for my sins. No matter what my circumstances my be, I will praise Your name, and I will pray with confidence that You hear me.

I close the door to the areas in my life where Satan has had a grip. I ask, God, that through the power of the Holy Spirit, You would give me strength to put all my concerns, hurts and trials into Your hands and trust Jesus as my Savior and Lord.

God, let me know the emotions that You feel toward me. Help me to gaze on Your beauty and experience Your love and joy so that I can understand how You sustain my heart. Thank you for making the way for me to know You in this way. Thank you that You will teach me how to pray. In Jesus' name, amen.

  E. Invite the Holy Spirit to visit your students, and ask if there is anyone who would like individual prayer. Pray for them and ask others to join you in praying for them when appropriate.

Student Journal and Notes

_____

_____

_____

_____

_____

_____

_____

_____

_____

_____

_____

_____

_____

_____

LESSON NINE: Giving Thanks to God

Biblical Foundation: 2 Chronicles 20:21
Song: "For the Lord is Good"

Objective: To show that praying a prayer of thanksgiving is the vital first step in releasing our hearts to worship Him. In giving thanks to God with our words, we are first acknowledging all He has done for us and given to us. Jesus' death and resurrection opened the way for us to have relationship with God. Now, we can pray with boldness in all things.

Resource Materials Needed:

- *Prayer* CD
- Sound system to play the CD
- Handouts of the lyrics to "For the Lord is Good"
- Your Bible and a Bible for each student
- Your journal and a journal for each student
- Handouts of the Apostolic Prayers

I. The Invitation: Into the Heart of God

This step will assist you in preparing to bring the heart of the message together with the heart of the music, while embracing God's heart for the students you will be teaching.

A. Listen to "For the Lord is Good" several times.

B. Consider the promises you believe God has given to you, or those spoken by others who have prayed for you.

C. As you listen to the song, reflect on situations in which your trust was not disappointed.

D. Ask the Holy Spirit to lead you in a prayer of thanksgiving for those promises and for God's faithfulness. Meditate on Psalm 136:1 as you thank Him.

E. What are some areas for which you are still praying and trusting? Ask the Lord to help you maintain a grateful heart regardless of your circumstances. Also, ask Him to keep bitterness from coming to your heart when things don't work out like you thought they would.

II. The Impartation: Into the Knowledge of God

This step will help you understand why the song was written and identify the main points to communicate from it. It will also help you gain insight into the biblical foundations of the lesson and the song as you consider the truths contained in each.

A. Main points to the song "For the Lord is Good"

1. This song endeavors to communicate the truth that acknowledging the Lord's goodness is our primary entrance into worship.

2. Giving thanks is not something that we do only when things are going well, but at all times, regardless of our circumstances.

3. God's goodness provides an answer to the accusations of the enemy. The enemy will always accuse the character of God, but Scripture refutes all of his accusations.

4. This song helps us remember that we should not accept the lie from the enemy that God is not good and His love does not last forever. As Hebrews 11:1 tells us, faith is our assurance of the things that we hope for, even though we haven't seen them yet with our eyes.

B. Biblical Foundation: Read, study, and meditate on 2 Chronicles 20:21.

And when he had consulted with the people, he appointed those who should sing to the Lord, and who should praise the beauty of holiness, as they went out before the army and were saying: "Praise the Lord, for His mercy endures forever."

Key Points to Remember

1. Jehoshaphat was the King of Judah. During all twenty-five years of his reign, he remained a lover of God, seeking Him in all things. He instituted many reforms in the land in regard to governing the people, but more importantly, he restored proper worship in the temple.

2. When Judah was invaded by the surrounding nations, Jehoshaphat exhorted his troops to be courageous because of their faith in God. Nothing offers stability to our hearts like unwavering faith in the power, mercy and faithfulness of God.

3. Jehoshaphat appointed the singers to go out before the army, believing that God would fight their battle for them, just as He said He would.

4. God did exactly what He promised. As the singers led the way in worship onto the battlefield, the Lord turned the opposing armies on one another, and Judah's enemies destroyed each other.

III. Preparation: Action Plan and Lesson Presentation Template

This step will help you develop an action plan to communicate the lesson using a template. This presentation template has been designed to assist you in organizing and presenting the material in the most effective manner.

Bear in mind all that you have considered and learned by contemplating the song and studying the lesson.

We, as teachers, are to serve our students; they are not to serve us. Remember that we do so in order that they may in turn serve God with a greater understanding of His ways in their lives. Be sensitive to the needs of the students, keeping in mind that God is faithful and good and knows them best.

"S.E.R.V.A.N.T." spelled out is:

S: "Share"—Share your life with your students.

E: "Example"—Be an example of the truth to them.

R: "Represent"—Represent Christ correctly to your students.

V: "Voice"—Help them learn to recognize God's voice.

A: "Authority"—Teach in the power of God with His authority.

N: "Needs"—Meet the needs of your students so that God is glorified.

T: "Train and Teach"—As you train and teach, do so rightly dividing the Word of God.

Prayer

Lesson Presentation Template

Theme: Prayer

Lesson: "Giving Thanks to God"

Lesson Biblical Foundation: 2 Chronicles 20:21

Song: "For the Lord is Good"

PART ONE: The Invitation

In this section, you will invite your students to know your heart for them to embrace the lesson you are teaching. Be transparent and reachable. Communicate your desire for them to experience from the lesson the heart and love God has for them.

A. Play "For the Lord is Good" several times.

B. Share with your students your responses to the following questions.

   a. How does saying a prayer of thanksgiving stir up your faith? What difference does gratitude make in the way you approach negative situations?

   b. Consider the times in your life that you wish you had more faith. Share one or more of these experiences with your students. How did you feel when you realized that you doubted God's faithfulness?

   c. Spend a few minutes sharing about the heart God has given you for your students. Choose a portion of Scripture from the Apostolic Prayers handout and pray it over them.

PART TWO: The Impartation

In this section, you will invite the students into the knowledge of God through His Word.

    A. Have the students open their Bibles. Read and study 2 Chronicles 20:21 with them.

    B. Talk about how Jehoshaphat probably felt. How can we be confident of victory in the Lord and still feel frightened because of our circumstances?

    C. Discuss how Judah's enemies were confounded by the faith that the army had in God. Ask your students to identify at least three attributes of God that make us confident that He can win a battle.

- #1

- #2

- #3

PART THREE: The Application

In this section, you will help the students identify areas of their lives where they can apply God's Word and experience His emotions.

Note: They should have their journals with them and be prepared to write in them.

A. Ask the students to identify areas in their life that make it hard to pray and sing of the goodness of the Lord.

B. Give them time to reflect on God's faithfulness to fight battles for them. Then, lead a corporate prayer, asking the Lord to give them courage and faith.

C. Ask them to share how they think a prayer of thanksgiving can silence the enemy and accusations that come against us.

D. Ask the students to journal what they think about Jehoshaphat's decision to send out the singers into battle. What would they have done if they were in his place?

E. Sending out singers in battle seems out of the ordinary. Have your students write one or two things in their journal that we as believers do or say that the world would think are "odd" or "not normal." How do they think God feels about it?

PART FOUR: The Impact

A. Play the song again. Give a copy of the lyrics to each student, and ask them to sing along.

B. Lead your students in prayer by waiting on the Lord and being silent before Him. Ask the students one at a time to pray for those who they know are having a hard time trusting in God's goodness.

C. Ask the students to pray one at a time, acknowledging God's goodness and faithfulness. Have them ask God to have His Word come alive in their hearts. Then have them meditate on God's goodness.

D. Print the following prayer and give a copy to each student. Pray it together out loud.

God, I rejoice in Your goodness. I praise You and I praise Your name. Your name is above all names.

Show me how to walk with understanding of your faithfulness. I desire to close the door to the areas in my life where Satan has had a grip. I ask, God, that through the power of the Holy Spirit, You would give me strength to put all my trust into Your hands and trust in Jesus as my Savior and Lord.

Thank you, God, for sending Your only Son to die for my sins. I know that this is the reason why I can worship You no matter what is going on in my life. When I'm happy, I will sing; and when I'm sad, I will sing. Even during times when I am afraid, I will lift my voice to praise You, Lord.

Thank you, God, for the way that You fight for me. Help me to trust You. Help me believe that You will always hear and answer me when I ask for help. In Jesus' name, amen.

E. Invite the Holy Spirit to visit your students and ask if there is anyone who would like individual prayer. Pray for them and ask others to join you in praying for them when appropriate.

Prayer

Student Journal and Notes

LESSON TEN: Jesus: The Lamb of God

Biblical Foundation: John 1:29–30 and 1 Peter 1:19–20
Song: "You Are Beautiful"

Objective: To help the students understand Jesus' identity as the Lamb of God and the forgiveness of sins, redemption, and eternal life that only He could provide. This lesson is designed to communicate this basis of Jesus' worth and beauty.

Resource Materials Needed:

- *Prayer* CD
- Sound system to play the CD
- Handouts of the lyrics to "You Are Beautiful"
- Your Bible and a Bible for each student
- Your journal and a journal for each student
- Handouts of the Apostolic Prayers

I. The Invitation: Into the Heart of God

This step will assist you in preparing to bring the heart of the message together with the heart of the music, while embracing God's heart for the students you will be teaching.

A. Listen to "You Are Beautiful" several times.

B. Mediate on John 1:29. Imagine what it was like to be there and actually see Jesus walking by and hearing John the Baptist exclaiming, "Behold! The Lamb of God who takes away the sin of the world!"

C. As you listen to the song, reflect on John saying in verse 30: "This is He of whom I said, 'After me comes a man that is preferred before me, for He was before me.'" Consider this statement in light of 1 Peter 1:19–20, that Jesus has been the Lamb since before the world was created.

D. Why does knowing Jesus as the Lamb of God make Him beautiful? Make a list of all the students you are teaching and pray for each one individually, asking God to reveal the beauty of the Lamb to them.

II. The Impartation: Into the Knowledge of God

This step will help you understand why the song was written and identify the main points to communicate from it. It will also help you gain insight into the biblical foundations of the lesson and the song as you consider the truths contained in each.

A. Main points to the song "You Are Beautiful"

1. This simple song expresses a heart of worship to Jesus, because no one is as worthy or as beautiful as He.

2. This song reminds us that nothing in this world can compare to the beauty of Jesus; though everything in this world will pass away, His beauty will always remain.

3. Despite the suffering that He experienced at the hands of men, He still loved. Therein lies His beauty: even in our ugliness, He loves us. "You Are Beautiful" stirs up our gratitude for Jesus' sacrifice and His loving nature.

4. This song is intended to demonstrate the ease with which we can express our adoration and devotion to Him.

B. Biblical Foundation: Read, study and meditate on John 1:29–30 and 1 Peter 1:19–20.

The next day, John saw Jesus coming toward him and said, "Behold! The Lamb of God who takes away the sin of the world! This is He of whom I said, 'After me comes a Man who is preferred before me, for He was before me.'" (John 1:29–30)

Key Points to Remember

1. In Hebrews 10, we see that sacrifices and burnt offerings were requirements of the Law. However, they were unable to forgive sins. Only the blood of Jesus Christ can blot out the sins of man so that they are no longer remembered.

2. John speaks here of Jesus as the atoning Savior.

3. Many people who saw Jesus thought that He was just a teacher or prophet, but with this statement, John is declaring that Jesus is much more—He is the great and only mediator and intercessor. His sinless life was given in place of our own in order to reconcile the world to God. (See also 1 John 3:5.)

...but with the precious blood of Christ, as of a lamb without blemish and without spot. He indeed was foreordained before the foundation of the world... (1 Peter 1:19–20)

III. Preparation: Action Plan and Lesson Presentation Template

This step will help you develop an action plan to communicate the lesson using a template. This presentation template has been designed to assist you in organizing and presenting the material in the most effective manner.

Bear in mind all that you have considered and learned by contemplating the song and studying the lesson.

We, as teachers, are to serve our students; they are not to serve us. Remember that we do so in order that they may in turn serve God with a greater understanding of His ways in their lives. Be sensitive to the needs of the students, keeping in mind that God is faithful and good and knows them best.

"S.E.R.V.A.N.T." spelled out is:

S: "Share"—Share your life with your students.

E: "Example"—Be an example of the truth to them.

R: "Represent"—Represent Christ correctly to your students.

V: "Voice"—Help them learn to recognize God's voice.

A: "Authority"—Teach in the power of God with His authority.

N: "Needs"—Meet the needs of your students so that God is glorified.

T: "Train and Teach"—As you train and teach, do so rightly dividing the Word of God.

Prayer

Lesson Presentation Template

Theme: Prayer

Lesson: "Jesus: The Lamb of God"

Lesson Biblical Foundation: John 1:29–30 and 1 Peter 1:19–20

Song: "You Are Beautiful"

PART ONE: The Invitation

In this section, you will invite your students to know your heart for them to embrace the lesson you are teaching. Be transparent and reachable. Communicate your desire for them to experience from the lesson the heart and love God has for them.

A. Play "You Are Beautiful" several times.

B. Share with your students your responses to the following questions.

   a. When and where did you give your life to the Lord? What were the circumstances?

   b. How hard is it for you to share your faith? Share a story of when you shared Jesus with someone even when you were afraid. How did you find the courage to do it?

   c. Are you praying for someone now to receive Christ? How do you pray for them?

   d. Spend a few minutes sharing about the heart God has given you for your students. Choose a portion of Scripture from the Apostolic Prayers handout and pray it over them.

PART TWO: The Impartation

In this section, you will invite the students into the knowledge of God through His Word.

A. Have the students open their Bibles. Read John 1:29–30 and 1 Peter 1:19–20 with them.

1. Ask your students to consider why Jesus came to Earth. What do they think is the most important thing that Jesus did during His ministry? Why? Discuss Jesus' role as the mediator and sacrifice.

2. Explain some of the historical context for using lambs as a sacrifice. Have the students think of at least three things they know about Jesus that would be reasons why He is the Lamb of God (gentleness, meekness, etc).

   - #1

   - #2

   - #3

3. Ask the students to list all of the things John the Baptist was probably thinking and feeling when he saw Jesus as the Lamb of God (joy, excitement, etc).

B. Jesus was the ultimate sacrifice and only mediator between God and man.

C. The lamb was the principle animal of sacrifice among the Jews. It was offered each morning and each evening.

D. Point out to the students that a lamb was also sacrificed on special religious days of significance. To the Jews, a lamb meant gentleness and innocence.

E. Discuss what kind of sacrifice it was for the Father to give His only Son to save the world. Ask the students about times when they gave up something that was very important to them.

PART THREE: The Application

In this section, you will help the students identify areas of their lives where they can apply God's Word and experience His emotions.

Note: They should have their journals with them and be prepared to write in them.

A. Discuss what it means to have a mediator, giving examples of people who might assume that role and situations when a mediator may be necessary.

B. Ask the students if they can think of a time when someone needed to speak on their behalf. Ask them to write the story in their journals.

C. Similarly, ask them to write about a time when they needed to be a mediator.

D. Lead the students in a corporate prayer, asking the Lord to give them words to share about Jesus with people who need to know Him.

PART FOUR: The Impact

A. Play the song again. Give a copy of the lyrics to each student and ask them to sing along. Also encourage them to speak out words of thanksgiving or declarations of the beauty of God.

B. Ask the students to pray one at a time for greater revelation of the beauty and worth of Jesus, the Lamb.

C. Have the students write out a prayer acknowledging God for all that He has revealed to them through this lesson.

D. Print the following prayer and give a copy to each student. Pray it together out loud.

Thank you, God, for sending Your only Son to die for my sins. Thank you for giving Jesus as the Lamb for sacrifice. Thank you for taking away my sins and making me clean so that I can be with You.

God, show me how to walk with a clear understanding of your beauty and sacrifice and to feel the emotions that You have for me. I close the door to the areas in my life where Satan has had a grip. I ask, God, that through the power of the Holy Spirit, You would give me strength to put all my trust into Your hands and fill me with the Holy Spirit and the power that is in the cross of Christ.

Jesus, I praise You because You are worthy. You are holy and beautiful. Thank you for being the mediator and giving Your life on my behalf. In Jesus' name, amen.

E. Invite the Holy Spirit to visit your students, and ask them if there is anyone who would like individual prayer. Pray for them and ask others to join you in praying for them when appropriate.

Student Journal and Notes

Song Lyrics

SONG OF JOY

Let me hear the song that You're singing over me, Lord (x4)

A song of love, a song of joy
You are singing over me (x2)

Let me hear the song
That You're singing over me, Lord (x2)

One with a voice like thunder
Singing over me (x2)

I want to hear what the angels hear
I want to see what the angels see (x2)

One with the voice like thunder
Singing over me (x2)

I want to hear what the angels hear
I want to see what the angels see (x2)

Carol Hall – Used with permission
©2004 Carol Hall/Forerunner Music (ASCAP)

BEFORE THE WORLD BEGAN

Before the world began
Before the world began
You knew me and You loved me (x2)

Jesus come into my heart
Come into my heart
Jesus come into my heart, today (x2)

Carol Hall – Used with permission

©2004 Carol Hall/Forerunner Music (ASCAP)

BANQUETING TABLE

He brought me to his banqueting table
His banner over me is love
I am my beloveds and he is mine
His banner over me is love

And we can feel the love of God in this place
We believe your goodness
We receive your grace
We delight ourselves at your table O God
You do all things well
Just look at our lives

His banner over you
His banner over me
His banner over us
Is love, love, love

Kevin Prosch – Used with permission
©1991 Mercy/Vineyard Publishing

DANCE WITH ME

Many songs will fade away
And few things will remain
Melodies and harmonies will change
Melodies and harmonies will change
But I'm hearing a new song
I'm hearing a new song

I'm beginning to hear the angels cry holy
Love song of God, rise in me
I'm surrounded by you here in your glory
Love song of God rise in me

I want to be romanced by the King of the ages
I don't want to sing of a passion I've never known
I want to get lost in the beauty of Jesus
To dance through the night around your throne

So dance with me
So dance with me

Evan Earwicker – Used with permission

©2002 Evan Earwicker/Unseen Obsession Music

THE LORD'S PRAYER

Our Father who is in heaven
Hallowed be your name (x2)

Let your kingdom come
Let your will be done
On earth as it is in heaven
Let your kingdom come

Our Father who is in heaven
Hallowed be your name (x2)

Give us our daily bread
And forgive us our sins
As we forgive those who sin against us
Let your kingdom come

And lead us not into temptation
But deliver us from evil (x2)

For yours is the kingdom
The power and the glory (x4)

For ever and ever (x6)

Carol Hall – Used with permission

©2004 Carol Hall/Forerunner Music (ASCAP)

SO GOOD TO ME

So good to me, my Lord, my friend
I see the love in your eyes
I hear the song you sing over me
You hold my heart, you hold my life

Wherever I go, whatever I do
I know that you're right there by my side
The hand of the Lord is so good to me
Wherever you lead that's where I'll go
I want to be right there by your side
The hand of the Lord is so good to me

I would have fainted
Unless I'd believed to see
The goodness of the Lord
In the land of the living

Chris DuPre – Used with permission

©2000 Heart of David Music. All rights reserved

Prayer

WIDE WIDE WORLD

Everybody come now
Everything that lives in this wide wide world
Everybody dance now
Before the living God in this wide wide world

Everybody praise now
Everybody shout in this wide wide world
Everybody sing now
Sing a brand new sing in this wide wide world

Sing to the Lord everybody
Everything that breathes

Everything that moves
Dance to the Lord everybody
Everything that breathes

Everything that moves
Heavens be glad earth rejoice
For the Lord is coming

To this wide wide world

Everybody praise the Lord

Written by David Ruis – Used with permission

©2000 Vineyard Songs Canada. Admin. in North America by Music Services O/B/O/ Vineyard Music Global, inc. (SOCAN)

EDEN ELYSIUM

Music by Fior Anam Visionary Sound

©2004 Fior Anam Visionary Sound. All rights reserved. Used with permission. International copyright secured

FOR THE LORD IS GOOD

For the Lord is good and his mercy endures forever (x4)
Hallelujah (hallelujah) (x4)
We believe that you are good (x8)

Carol Hall – Used with permission

©2004 Carol Hall/Forerunner Music (ASCAP)

YOU ARE BEAUTIFUL

You are beautiful in your holiness
Jesus, Jesus
I will lift my hands
I will lift my voice
Jesus, Jesus

I will worship you
Just let me love you Jesus, Jesus

There is no one as holy
There is no one as worthy
There is no one as beautiful as the lamb of God
As the lamb of God

Carol Hall – Used with permission

©2004 Carol Hall/Forerunner Music (ASCAP)

Age Group Characteristics and Communication Tips

I.   Basic age group characteristics to remember when adapting a lesson to be age-group–appropriate:

     A.   8-Year-Olds

          1.   They may spread themselves too thin and things may wind up in a mess.

          2.   Relationships between parents and children may get complicated.

          3.   They fair well with other siblings.

          4.   School is important because friends are there.

          5.   About God: children should learn that God is all-powerful, all-knowing, is everywhere, is with them at all times, loves them and wants to have a relationship with them.

a. God wants them to know that each of them is special in His sight. God cares for and loves their families too.

b. God wants them to talk with Him in prayer every day.

c. God always answers prayer with "yes" or "no" or "wait." He provides all they need. He can be trusted for all things.

6. About Jesus: children should learn that Jesus is the Son of God who came to Earth to be our Savior and die for our sins.

a. Jesus wants all people to come to Him as their Lord and Savior. Jesus is the only way to God and Heaven.

b. Jesus wants to take sins from our lives. Jesus was perfect and never did anything wrong.

c. Jesus rose from the dead and now lives in Heaven. He is preparing a place for us to live with Him in Heaven.

d. Jesus will return some day to take us home forever. He loves us and is our best friend. Jesus wants us to love and obey Him and do the things that He taught us to do.

7. About the Holy Spirit: children should learn that when Jesus went to Heaven, He sent the Holy Spirit as our comforter and teacher.

a. The Holy Spirit will give us the power and desire to do the will of the Father.

b. Through the Holy Spirit we can participate in the things that Jesus did and told us to do.

c. The Holy Spirit will speak to our hearts and show us where there is sin.

d. He will help us worship the Lord and give us things to say to the Lord.

e. It is through the work of the Holy Spirit that we will see healing, miracles and changed lives.

f. Through the power of the Holy Spirit others will come to know Jesus.

8. About the Bible: children should learn that it is God's Word to His children.

a. The Bible tells us what God wants and how we are to live our lives in relationship with Him.

b. The Bible reveals God's perfect love for us. It tells us about how He related to other people. It tells us about who we are and why we were created.

c. The Bible has two major parts called the Old Testament and the New Testament. There are sixty-six books in the Bible.

d. We should read and memorize it so that we will be built up and strengthened by God's Word to us.

9. About home and parents: parents have rules for them to follow, but God also has rules for them to follow.

a. God wants to be at home in their household and to be in authority there.

b. God wants to restore their home when there is sin present.

c. They can go to the Father in prayer to receive help and restoration for their homes and for their relationships.

d. They can be ambassadors in their homes to any non-believers living there.

10. About church: children should learn that they come to church to learn about God, Jesus and the Holy Spirit.

a. Church is a place to see friends and enjoy others. It is a place where they can feel loved, warm and safe.

    b. Church is a place where other people really show their love and care.

    c. Church is God's house and is a place where we come to worship God and pray for one another.

    d. Church is more than a building; it is also the people who make up the church.

    e. They can give money to the church to help buy things and provide outreach to others.

11. About others: children should learn that God loves all people and He wants them to show love and compassion for others.

    a. God wants them to lead others to Jesus in love and in deed. He wants them to pray for others, even those who may be their enemies.

    b. God wants them to be able to turn the other cheek and do good to those who mistreat them.

    c. God wants them to forgive.

    d. God wants them to share with and give to others.

12. About other biblical concepts: children should learn that angels are messengers from God sent to tell people when Jesus was born, to protect God's children, and to do God's work.

    a. Fallen angels are the demons who work for Satan.

    b. Satan will do anything within his power to cause us to sin, and he will tempt us to disobey.

B.   9-Year-Olds: for the most part, they like school. They are apt to forget things unless reminded.

    1.   They are critical of things they think they could do better.

C.   10-Year-Olds: they are fond of friends and like to tell people who they are.

    1.   Simple companionship rather than competition motivates this group.

    2.   Physical stamina is at a higher level.

D.   11-Year-Olds: peers continue to take up more of their time at this stage.

    1.   They can often seem intense and can fly into a rage at short notice.

    2.   Acceptance is very important to them.

E.   12-Year-Olds

    1.   About God: children should learn that God is all powerful, all knowing, is everywhere, and is with them at all times.

        a.   He loves them and wants to have a relationship with them. He wants them to know that each of them is special in His sight. God cares for and loves their families too.

        b.   God wants them to talk with Him in prayer every day. He always answers prayer with "yes," "no" or "wait." He provides all they need. He can be trusted for all things.

        c.   God desires their worship. He wants them to trust Him in all their needs and problems, and be thankful for all He has done and is doing in their lives. God wants them to be obedient to their parents and those in authority.

d. God wants them to share His love with others. He wants them to go to His Word to learn about Him, to hear His voice through the Word, and to learn how to live their lives for Him.

2. About Jesus: children should learn that He wants to be their Lord and Savior.

    a. Through His death on the Cross, Jesus conquered sin and death once and for all. He can and desires to forgive them of their sins. Jesus will grant salvation to all who ask, and He loves them even when they sin.

    b. Jesus wants them to be His disciples, follow Him and do His works that He commanded us to do. Jesus is the only way to God and Heaven. He loves them and is their best friend.

    c. Jesus wants them to love and obey Him with all of their hearts, souls, minds, and strength.

3. About the Holy Spirit: children should learn that when Jesus went to Heaven, He sent the Holy Spirit as our comforter and teacher.

    a. The Holy Spirit will give us the power and desire to do the Father's will. Through the Holy Spirit we can participate in the things that Jesus did and told us to do.

    b. The Holy Spirit will speak to our hearts and show us where there is sin. He will help us worship the Lord and give us things to say to the Lord. It is through the work of the Holy Spirit that we will see healings, miracles, and changed lives.

    c. Through the power of the Holy Spirit others will come to know Jesus. They can operate in the gifts of the Spirit. God wants us to live by the fruit of the Spirit.

4. About the Bible: children should learn that it is God's Word to them and it will reveal the truth to all their questions.

    a. The Bible tells them what God wants for them to know and how they are to live their lives for Him.

b. The Bible reveals His perfect love for them. It tells them about how He related to others and showed mankind that He desired to bring us back to Him.

c. It tells them about who they are and why they were created. The Bible was written by the hands of men chosen by God and inspired by the Holy Spirit to write what God told them.

d. The Bible has two major parts called the Old Testament and New Testament. There are sixty-six books in the Bible.

e. The gospels (Matthew, Mark, Luke and John) tell of the life and works of Jesus. They should know the groupings of the other major writings of the Bible.

f. They should read and memorize the Scriptures so they will be strengthened by God's Word to them.

5. About home and parents: children should learn that God gave them parents to care for them and bring them up in the ways of the Lord.

a. If their parents are non-believers, they are to still honor and obey their parents. Our parents love us and we should love them.

b. God cares for their families and each member in their families. Parents have rules to follow and we should obey them.

c. God wants to be the authority in each household. Children should know that they can ask God for help in restoring their family situations, and that God cares very much about their family situations.

6. About church: children should learn that church is a place to worship and to learn about God.

a. It is a place for them to be equipped and trained as a part of the Christian body. Church should be a place where they feel secure and loved.

7.   About others: children should learn that God loves all people equally, whether or not they believe in Christ.

   a. God wants children to learn how to show love and compassion for people.

   b. They should know how to lead others to Christ, and to pray for friends and peers. Children should know that they can minister to others.

8.   About other biblical concepts: children should learn about Bible truths, including the nature of sin, the forgiveness of God through Christ, baptism, communion, death and Heaven.

   a. They should be taught about Satan, and how he is the tempter and deceiver.

   b. They should know that God has power over all things, including the works of Satan. Children should also learn about Christ's Second Coming, and how that affects their lives.

II.   Basic communication tips

The following outline may help you in better understanding how to communicate with your children and students. Each child should be treated as an individual. They may react in different ways to different types of communication.

A. Respect children.

B. Talk to children.

   1. Do not interrogate them.

   2. Do not conduct an interview.

   3. Do not preach.

   4. Simply hold a conversation with them.

   5. Make them feel better about themselves.

C. Listen to children.

    1. Get on their level.

        i. Physically

        ii. In vocabulary—use words they can understand

    2. Listen completely to the whole story.

    3. Listen for attitudes, values, and feelings.

D. Simple reminders:

    1. Treat every child with respect and as an individual.

    2. Be sincere, as with a friend.

    3. Do not be impatient.

    4. Do not jump to obvious answers or conclusions.

    5. Do not be too quick to quote the Bible or give simple answers.

    6. Balance talking and listening.

    7. Evaluate your conversation.

Sometimes we experience difficulty in relating to or communicating with a child. The following is a list of some possible roadblocks to effective communication.

A. Verbal Roadblocks

    1. Ordering or commanding. Examples: "Get down" or "Stop that."

    2. Admonishing. Examples: "You should…" or "You ought to…"

    3. Judging.

i. Positive judging. Example: "You are right."

   ii. Negative judging. Example: "You made a mistake."

 4. Using logic. Example: "What you need to know is…"

 5. Name calling. Examples: "Lazy" or "selfish" or "stupid"

 6. Interpreting. Example: "You feel this way because…"

 7. Interrogating and probing. Example: Asking "Who, what, why, when, where"

 8. Advising. Example: "I'll tell you what to do…"

 9. Comparing. Example: "When I was your age…"

B. Non-verbal Roadblocks

 1. Preaching tone of voice

 2. Condescending tone

 3. Looking away, looking bored

 4. Fixed smile

 5. No eye contact

About the Children's Equipping Center
International House of Prayer in Kansas City

The Children's Equipping Center (CEC) has set out to establish a culture that equips children to live fully devoted to God. The CEC's highest priority is to pass on to the next generation the values, programs and practices that are foundational to IHOP-KC and its environment of 24-hour-a-day, night and day prayer and worship.

The Children's Equipping Center develops opportunities for children of all ages to develop and be released into their gifts as musicians, singers, artists, dancers and intercessors. It seeks to enable them to understand the power of the Holy spirit through praying, healing, preaching, teaching, giving to the poor, and reaching the lost through evangelism and missions.

> "We are committed in these days ahead to doing whatever we can to help young people pursue a lifelong passion for Jesus. It is the desire of Lenny and Tracy La Guardia and their staff who serve the Children's Equipping Center that young people experience the power and ministry of the Holy Spirit and walk out their lives knowing that they are truly a 'Friend of the Bridegroom.' Lenny and Tracy have dedicated more than twenty years of their lives to children, leaders and churches all over the world. I encourage you to allow the Children's Equipping Center to bless you as it has the children and families here in Kansas City."

—Mike Bickle, Director
International House of Prayer, Kansas City, Missouri

CEC Directors Lenny & Tracy La Guardia

For two decades, Lenny and Tracy La Guardia have devoted their lives to equipping, empowering, enabling and mobilizing today's young people, parents, and leaders by communicating and putting into place Kingdom of God truths and relevant strategies for ministry to children today.

The La Guardias' passion for mobilizing this generation of children and young people to walk in the fullness of Christ and in the power of the Holy Spirit has taken them all over the world as speakers and consultants to thousands. In their senior staff capacity at the International House of Prayer Missions Base in Kansas City, under the leadership of Mike Bickle, they direct and oversee all local, national and international ministries relating to children and teens. They have been married 25 years and have five children: Lenny, Leatha, Andrea, Adrienne and Shontavion. To request that Lenny or Tracy speak or consult at your church or event, or to host a Children's Prophetic Leadership Summit, please e-mail your invitation to equipchildren@ihop.org.

Children's Equipping Center Annual Events

National Children's Equipping Conference
Held every September, this conference seeks to further CEC's goal of equipping a generation to receive and experience God's love and to love God in return. This conference also fulfills CEC's call to gather parents and others who lead children and desire to equip an end-time army of forerunners.

Like never before, we have the opportunity and responsibility to train, equip and prepare young forerunners to passionately pursue the Lord, and to release them into their God-given destinies. This yearly event covers topics that impact and change the hearts and lives of parents, as well as children's and teen's pastors, leaders, and teachers. Teaching tracks and breakout sessions are designed to equip attendees with strategies and truths that will help them do their part in releasing this generation in prayer, praise, power and the prophetic. There are additional breakout sessions on leadership and resource development, ministry to toddlers and preschoolers, releasing children in worship and praise, the ministry of the Holy Spirit, and signs and wonders.

Children of all ages are welcome, though no childcare is available. There is a children's equipping track for ages 6-12. Ages 1-5 are welcome to attend the main sessions with their parents. There is a pre-conference lunch held on the Friday before the conference. For costs, conference details, registration and a sample schedule, please visit *www.IHOP.org.*

Releasing Children in Power & Praise
This two-day seminar held three times a year is an opportunity for parents and leaders to be equipped side-by-side with their children and youth for worship and intercession. Explore the gifts and power of the Holy Spirit that are released when His people lift up God's praises. The weekend includes teaching and practical experience for children and adults in the Harp and Bowl model of prayer. There is no childcare provided. For costs, seminar details, registration and a sample schedule, please visit *www.IHOP.org.*

Leadership Summit: Changing Paradigms of Ministry to Children
The goal of this summit is for leaders, pastors and parents to get refreshed in the prayer room and equipped and retooled for their ministries. Summits have a relaxed atmosphere with more personal ministry and teaching and are held quarterly. There is no childcare provided. There are group discounts. For costs, details and registration, please visit *www.IHOP.org.*

Signs & Wonders Camps

These camps are offered at locations in Kansas City, Mississippi and Colorado. Children 8 to 12 years old receive training, teaching and practical experience walking with the Holy Spirit and ministering in power. This is coupled with the fun and recreation of summer camp. There are group discounts available and costs include food, lodging, teaching workbook and more. For costs, details, dates and downloadable registration forms, please visit *www.IHOP.org.*

Summer Teen Intensive

Held each summer, the intensive is a three-week program aimed at equipping teens in prophetic worship, intercession, intimacy with Jesus, and the great commission. Group discounts are available. Tuition includes all meals, lodging, materials and more. For costs, details, dates and a downloadable application, please visit *www.ihop.org.*